THE
BUSH FAMILY
COOKBOOK

★

Ariel De Guzman

A LISA DREW BOOK

SCRIBNER
New York   London   Toronto   Sydney

A LISA DREW BOOK/SCRIBNER
1230 Avenue of the Americas
New York, NY 10020

SCRIBNER and design are trademarks of Macmillan Library Reference USA, Inc.,
used under license by Simon & Schuster, the publisher of this work.

For information about special discounts for bulk purchases,
please contact Simon & Schuster Special Sales:
1-800-456-6798 or business@simonandschuster.com

A LISA DREW BOOK is a trademark of Simon & Schuster, Inc.

Set in Adobe Caslon

DESIGNED BY ERICH HOBBING

Manufactured in the United States of America

1   3   5   7   9   10   8   6   4   2

Library of Congress Cataloging-in-Publication Data is available.

ISBN-13: 978-0-7432-8776-0
ISBN-10: 0-7432-8776-2

For my loving wife,
Elizabeth,
whose unwavering commitment to our family
has contributed to our success.

CONTENTS

THE
BUSH FAMILY
COOKBOOK

★

GEORGE BUSH

Foreword

The United States Navy sent Ariel to us in 1981, when I was Vice President of the United States. We could not imagine then that Ariel would still be with us 24 years later and become like a member of our family.

When I was elected President in 1988, Ariel was one of the staffers from the Vice President's residence that I brought to the White House with me. By that time he has already spoiled me by his anticipation of every single need. He has been through all the ups and downs with me – from the tranquility of Camp David; to that now famous meeting with Mikhail Gorbachev in the stormy seas off Malta; through the turmoil and tension of Iraq's invasion of Kuwait, followed by the triumphant end of Desert Storm; and then of course the 1992 election.

One of the things that was toughest for Barbara and me when we left the White House was leaving behind so many people for whom we cared a great deal, including Ariel. So imagine how thrilled we were when Ariel called us in 1995 to tell us he was retiring from the Navy and wondered if he could come join us in Houston. Ten years later, he's still with us and I honestly am not sure how we would survive without him. I am so glad that Ariel has decided to share his story, not to mention his great recipes, with all of you. His is truly a great American story.

Barbara Bush

"As I wrote in my recent book, *Reflections*, my hero, Ariel, arrived not on a white horse, but via the U.S. Navy. Ariel is a miracle man, not only as a "good soldier" (Navy man), but also as a great chef. He may even be a saint!

George has not slowed down at all, even after his 80th birthday in 2004. He significantly increased his social schedule and we now receive and entertain a large number of our friends at Walker's Point, at his Library at College Station, Texas, at our home and his office in Houston. Ariel finds himself in more tight spots now than ever before. There were seven professional Navy men working side by side at the Vice President House and even more military staff at the White House, but for years now, Ariel has *single-handedly* kept up with George and my many demands and has always delivered without fail. I spoke the truth in my book about him before. I gladly reiterate my support of Ariel now."

April 2005

JEB BUSH
GOVERNOR OF THE STATE OF FLORIDA

Ariel has always been there for Colu, my children and me each time we visited with my parents. My youngest son, Jeb Jr., spent almost every summer with his Gampy and Ganny at Walker's Point and Ariel became like a secondary summer guardian to Jeb during his summer vacations. George P., my oldest son, was married at Kennebunkport and - as promised - Ariel provided him with a groom's cake almost as big as the bride's cake!

Ariel watched my children grow into the wonderful people they are today. He takes great care of my parents and selflessly extends himself to make our visits to both Houston and Maine even more special. Ariel's genuine and sincere acts of kindness have had a positive effect on my family and me.

-- John Ellis "Jeb" Bush, Governor of Florida

INTRODUCTION

I was born on March 3, 1948, in Paniqui, Tarlac, a quaint little town located seventy miles north of Manila, Philippines. My father was a public land surveyor, and my mother a respected elementary school teacher. But it was my older brother I idolized, because as a sailor in the U.S. Navy, he regularly sent us portions of his pay, American dollars, which were worth more than what my mother made in pesos. I was in high school when my brother joined the Navy, and I wanted to follow in his footsteps. In addition, the people in my small hometown believed America was a land of opportunity and I, too, dreamed that a better life might be waiting for me in America. Those able to travel or relocate to the United States were considered very lucky.

I applied to the U.S. Navy after high school graduation, but only a handful of recruits were selected every month. In the interim, I went to college, due in part to an athletic scholarship in pole-vaulting and as a high jumper and long jumper. I never failed to submit my monthly application to the Navy, even as my college career entered its third year, with a major in Education. At the end of my junior year, my perseverance paid off. I received my long-awaited letter from the Navy, and after passing all entry exams, I was sworn in on August 18, 1969.

I soon found out that even a college-educated immigrant could only elect to perform a Stewardsman (SD) position in the U.S. Navy. Happily, that was the job I accepted. After all, it was a fresh start for me. So I had no complaints about the system.

In the beginning, I performed less demanding and noncritical job functions, since I was still petitioning to become a U.S. citizen. I understood that regardless of my previous work experience and proven capabilities, I had to start from the bottom and work my way up. Not a stranger to hard work and perseverance, I took on my military assignments and did the best job I could.

My primary duty as a Stewardsman was to cater to officers onboard Navy ships. Ashore, I served as a Stewardsman at various bachelor officers' quarters. I cooked and served military personnel ranging from commissioned and warrant officers to the highest-ranking admirals in the fleet.

The dining menu in the officers' wardroom was more elaborate than the enlisted dining facility menu. While enlisted personnel meals were based solely on preplanned cycle menus, officer meals were based on gourmet-style cuisine. This work detail is where the foundation of my gourmet cooking skills developed.

Cooking for officers allowed me to stretch my creative muscles in the realm of gourmet cuisine. I learned all aspects of food service management. With my inherited artistic ability and increasing interest in the trade, I trained to become a military gourmet cook.

The training I received as a Stewardsman was equivalent to the skill set of a garde-manger, chef-educator, sous chef, pastry chef—or even an executive chef in a civilian workplace. But military servicemen have no claim to formal civilian titles. The trade-off was that shortly after my training was completed, I increased in military rank.

My ambition to learn, perform well, and excel in my job helped define the skill set that framed the remainder of my military career.

EXPANDING MY HORIZONS

In my early years in the Navy, I was assigned duty onboard the USS *Prairie* (AD 15)—homeported in San Diego, California. This was convenient for me, especially since I had family nearby in San Francisco. On one of my visits to the Bay area, I reunited with and later married my beautiful childhood sweetheart, Elizabeth Embry Cancio.

Elizabeth remained in the San Francisco area until our son, Ariel Jr., was born. Soon after, I was reassigned to another destroyer tender (an auxiliary support ship), the USS *Piedmont* (AD-17)—homeported in Long Beach, California. Our second child, Melody, was born while I was stationed there.

Within the first five years of my naval career, we moved to five different locations, from one coast of the United States to the other. My wife, Ariel Jr., and Melody grew accustomed to living the nomad military family life.

By this time, my petition to become a U.S. citizen was approved. This expanded the range of my military job opportunities. Choosing a new military rating would have meant a fresh start in another line of work, but I declined the offer since my advancement to a higher rank was pending. After everything I learned and the skills I developed as a Stewardsman, I was reluctant to start over in another field of training. Besides, I had learned to love the job.

MERGING TECHNIQUES

On January 1, 1975, both Stewardsman and Commissaryman ratings were abolished. The two former ratings were merged into one, and all former personnel became Mess Management Specialists (MS).

For a former Stewardsman, this presented the new challenge of adopting the cooking techniques of former Commissarymen. It meant learning the business of mass food production. I learned to put more emphasis on quantity but was taught never to sacrifice quality.

After a three-year tour onboard aircraft carrier USS *Enterprise* (CVN—65) from 1977 to 1979, I became a proficient Mess Management Specialist, adding skills to my repertoire.

Page 4, January 23, 1981

Local sailor to cook for VP

**Story and photo
by SA Joni Owens**

MS1 Ariel DeGuzman, attached to USS Fairfax County, has discovered that one never knows where travels in the Navy might lead.

DeGuzman received word from Washington, D.C. last July that he was being considered for a position as a cook for the new administration at the White House in 1981. A later message informed him he had been chosen as one of seven cooks for the incoming Vice President.

Born in the Philippines, DeGuzman joined the Navy in 1969. He has spent a year on board USS Fairfax County where he serves as leading petty officer, records keeper (food service officer), wardroom supervisor, and assistant galley supervisor.

The story of DeGuzman's future assignment began to unfold last November after his ship had left on a training cruise for West Africa. During the cruise an interview for his potential job was arranged in Washington.

"I was flown back to the States on December 2, 1980 — 16 days ahead of my ship's destined date of return — and spent three days in Washington. I helped with two receptions in which a lot of Senators were present, and I also met then-Vice President Mondale," he said. DeGuzman returned to Little Creek and rejoined USS Fairfax County upon its return a week later.

DeGuzman is now awaiting a final set of orders and he will be on his way to Washington as a cook for Vice President George Bush. Government housing has been arranged for him and his family at Bowling Air Force Base. "I'm very excited about this and I think my wife is even more excited than I am," said DeGuzman.

DeGuzman credits two Navy men with assisting him on his climb to the Washington position. "I owe a lot of thanks to Cdr. R.H. Heidt, Commanding Officer of USS Fairfax County, and Ltjg. Ray Cook, my division officer, for this job. They helped me any way they could," he said.

WASHINGTON-BOUND COOK MS1 DeGuzman helps with dinner preparations in the wardroom galley on board USS Fairfax County. MS1 DeGuzman will soon leave the ship to become a cook for the Vice President.

In my training as a copperman, for instance, I was taught how to use 120-gallon copper steamers to prepare food. No, I don't intend to include in this cookbook a recipe on how to prepare spaghetti with meatballs in a tublike steamer, using a 6-foot paddle as a stirrer! I did become very adept in butchering after I completed that training. And from my experience as a spudlockerman, I handled a vast array of fresh fruits and vegetables and prepared a multitude of salads. My experience as a spudlockerman gave me opportunities to showcase my fine-tuned knowledge of artistic vegetable carving and garnitures with the ship's five thousand crew members.

AN OPPORTUNITY OF A LIFETIME

Mess Management Specialists were often recruited, screened, and selected to serve on special assignments, including gourmet cuisine preparation in the White House, the presidential retreat at Camp David, the official residence of the U.S. Vice President, and Chief of Naval Operations quarters. I was one of thousands of former Stewards nominated. In 1980, while onboard USS *Fairfax County* (LST-1193) homeported in Little Creek, Virginia, I received a message from the Bureau of Naval Personnel, Washington, D.C.

The message read that I was being considered as a possible candidate for duty in the White House Mess. My initial reaction was "Huh? Me? White House? What? Why me? How?" I couldn't understand why I was even being considered for such a prominent position, especially when I hadn't applied for it.

I was a Second Class Petty Officer (E-5) at the time and knew nothing about the special assignment. It was only then that I learned such assignments even existed. There are really Navy cooks serving at the White House? I thought to myself.

I called the detailing officer for special assignments who informed me that announcements were sent out to thousands of possible candidates like me, and because it was only an announcement, it was nothing to be excited about.

After the initial elimination process, the selection list narrowed to approximately three hundred candidates. I was informed that I was still on the list. At that point, I cleared my mind of the possibility of being picked. My family and I went on with our normal lives, expecting nothing more than the usual routine. Not anticipating leaving the area, my wife and I bought our first home in Virginia Beach. Within a few months, we planned to enlarge the family.

Elizabeth was carrying our third child when I left for an African diplomatic cruise. Our Navy ship was in Niger, Africa, when I received a message requesting my immediate return. I had an interview scheduled with the military supervisors at the official residence of Walter Mondale, the U.S. Vice President.

I flew to Washington, D.C., completely puzzled and filled with questions. What happened to the three hundred candidates? Why were they calling for me now? Why the Vice President's House? What happened to the White House? And why was I being put in this position? What exactly was going on?"

THE BEST OF THE BEST

I met with seven Chief Petty Officers. All U.S. Navy Cooks. All former Stewards. Walking in, I knew these were the U.S. Navy's best, put together in one place.

At the time of my interview, all seven of them were busily preparing dinner for Vice President Mondale and his visiting dignitaries. I quietly watched the action taking place in the kitchen. Everyone performed flawlessly. Smooth and precise. As if each movement had been practiced to perfection. In that instant, I felt immensely scared. I felt unworthy—as if I didn't belong there.

Who could imagine that a simple Navy sailor could mingle with the elite crowd in Washington, D.C.? I thought to myself.

I sat in awe. But in the midst of my fear, there was also excitement at the thought of being inside the official residence of the Vice President of the United States. I was a sailor who honestly wished his shipmates "could see me now."

THE PROCESS OF ELIMINATION

In the course of my interview, all of my questions were answered. Out of three hundred candidates, the final seven were chosen for assignment at the White House Mess. They told me all seven candidates survived the election process because our military records had shown superb performance and were immaculately clean.

I asked, "If I was picked for assignment at the White House Mess with the other six finalists, then why am I being interviewed here at the Vice President's House?"

I was told that since Chief Emilio Edura was transferring, they needed an immediate replacement. Instead of starting a new list of recruits and a new process of elimination, the Military Support Group of the Vice President's Office acquired the military records and files of the seven primary candidates for the White House Mess. Out of seven candidates came three finalists. The other two had been interviewed ahead of me, since I had had to be flown back from Niger.

Master Chief Rodriguez asked if I would accept the job if I were selected.

"I sure will," I said. It was the final question of my interview.

I went home to Virginia Beach with a somewhat heavy heart. After I gave my family lots of hugs and kisses—happy to be home and together again—I discussed the switch from the White House to the Vice President's residence with my wife.

"Was I the worst of the seven finalists? Is that really the reason they sent me to the Vice President's House instead of the White House?"

Elizabeth hushed me by saying, "The supervisors picked the strongest out of seven. They settled for the best and gave the rest away."

To rid myself of the looming feeling of being unwanted at the White House, I asked Chief Florencio Chan how they determined the final candidates. Chan said he was provided records and files of all seven candidates. He studied each record at home over the weekend. The following weekend, Senior Chief Herman Capati brought the seven records home and studied them. The following day, Master Chief Rodriguez asked the two section leaders to write the name of the candidate of their choice on a piece of paper. The two section leaders wrote down their selection, folded their slip of paper in half, and handed it to Master Chief Rodriguez. Rodriguez looked them over and announced that both chose the same person. Me.

Chief Chan further clarified that their choice had been made before I was called back from Africa. The interview was simply to determine if I was willing to accept the job. That was the easy part.

The hard part was waiting for the Security Clearance Department to complete my background investigation. The investigation had to be extended all the way back to my hometown in the Philippines, so it took them a while. I was told they spoke with my high school principal, our local church minister, and our town chief of police.

By the end of September 1981, my permanent change of station orders arrived, and I was released from my last command. The house my wife and I purchased was placed on the market. Elizabeth was due to deliver our third child; I requested a slight delay on my reporting period, and it was granted. On October 14, 1981, my son Orville was born. Our new baby boy was a mere six days old when we traveled to Washington, D.C., but we were happy. With my new shore duty, my young family was finally together.

INSIDE WASHINGTON'S BELTWAY

Relocation was a breeze. The Vice President's household staff took care of nearly everything. I felt so welcome by the same friendly group.

Vice President George Herbert Walker Bush and Mrs. Barbara Pierce Bush were my new bosses. My direct contact with them was incomparable to anything I ever experienced. To be in their presence was overwhelming. I admired them both so completely that, at the time, I felt as though I was choked up from happiness whenever I was near them. It felt like a dream come true for me.

Photo opportunity with the Bush brothers on January 27, 1984, a few months before I left the Vice President's House for military duties in Guam. Front row: Romeo Cruz, Rudolfo Arca, Orlando Frilles, and Herman Capati. Back row: John Ellis Bush (Jeb), George W., Marvin, Neil Bush, and yours truly.

In my new work location, the first thing my counterparts taught me was never to address them by their military rank, but by first name only. This was generous, considering I was the lowest-ranking member of the team who was not a chief.

All of us had our own gourmet cuisine specialties, which spanned the globe. I brought my knowledge of cake decorating, vegetable carving for garnishment, butter and ice sculpting, and the willingness to learn and be as skillful as the rest of the team. Teamwork was the motto; we became one solid team. We carried the load together, and each person worked just as hard as the next.

No job was so big that we couldn't handle it. We tackled receptions for officials and nonofficials and personal events ranging from a simple tea for two to huge tent parties for five hundred guests. I was exposed to more advanced and sophisticated food preparation and thoroughly benefited from the staff's willingness to show me the ropes.

UNNECESSARY MOVE

After three years of duty in the Vice President's House, I made the heavyhearted decision to move my family out of the city; both my wife and oldest son were experiencing severe allergies and asthma. The doctor recommended reassignment of military duty, preferably a tour in a tropical destination. So I took an assignment as head of the dining facility in U.S. Naval Station, Guam. When my family's allergy condition didn't improve, further research suggested that their medical issues stemmed from my cigarette smoking. I was on sea duty during most of my young family's life, so I didn't realize that my new shore duty meant exposing them to my secondhand cigarette smoke. Talk about shooting yourself in the foot! I immediately kicked my indoor smoking habit and managed to slowly taper off cigarette use altogether.

I wrote to the Vice President and Mrs. Bush in 1986 expressing my desire to return to my job, and they were elated to accept. I vividly remember the sweet voice of Mrs. Bush's first line of greeting, "Welcome home." I had been away for twenty-one months.

GOING WITH THE FLOW

Vice President Bush was serving his second term under President Reagan when I returned. It felt as if I had never left at all, but I still tripled my efforts to catch up. I was filled in on what I missed and taught new skills the team acquired in my absence.

In 1988, Vice President Bush was elected the 41st President of the United States. During one of the victory parties held at the Vice President's House, actor and comedian Dan Aykroyd asked the newly elected President if he planned to take his household staff to the White House with him. President Bush said no, it's not how the system works. All the Vice President's House staff are assigned to stay and serve the incoming Vice President, in this case Dan Quayle. President Bush added that the White House was fully manned by military personnel, who

at the time were serving President Reagan and would stay on to serve the President-elect. With that knowledge, we prepared for the transition and arrival of Vice President Quayle, who was due to move into the Vice President's House just before inauguration day. President-elect and Mrs. Bush were to move temporarily into Blair House before moving into the White House.

In the interim, Paula Rendon, Mrs. Bush's longtime personal house aide, had a problem. She had become attached to the Vice President's House, and the thought of moving to the White House terrified her. Paula claimed she didn't know anyone at the White House, and she would rather retire and go home to Houston. Mr. Bush wouldn't have it. He asked, "If some of the boys go with you to the White House, will you go then?" Paula's answer was "Yes, of course."

She was told to ask who among the boys would like to go to the White House. She must have asked two or three of the guys who were on duty that day, but they all said, "No, thank you." During my duty the following morning, Paula asked me if I wanted to go with her to Blair House. She added that she also asked the guys who were on duty the other day and was turned down. I felt sorry for her and also was puzzled by the rejections. Why don't they want to help her move to Blair House? I wondered.

"Sure, I'll help you take your bags. I'll go with you," I answered. Why not? I thought to myself. I had duty that day anyway. Besides, I'd never been to Blair House and was curious to see how the place looked. Orlando Frilles, who was on duty with me that day, also accepted. Paula was elated by our acceptance, and she said she would tell Mr. Bush as soon as he came home from his office.

Upon Mr. Bush's arrival, which was close to dinnertime, I went up to their study to offer drinks before dinner. Mr. Bush said, "I'm glad you are going to the White House with us. We are moving out of here in two days. You and Orlando should be ready to move to the White House."

Wow! I thought, where did that come from? I'm moving to the White House? I thought we were asked only to help move and carry bags to Blair House? I went home still puzzled, because we all heard Mr. Bush tell Dan Aykroyd about how the system works. Where will they place us? Wasn't every job at the White House Mess still occupied by the same military staff that worked for the outgoing administration?

Orlando and I both agreed that we would not let Mr. and Mrs. Bush hear about the mixed-up bag-carrying mission to Blair House, and we assumed that our selection was of Paula's choosing and not because the two of us were the best among the seven Mess Specialists at the Vice President's House. There was no favoritism among us on Paula's part. Orlando and I just happened to say yes to Paula's plea for help. Carry bags? She just asked the question in her own sweet way. The message was simply interpreted differently.

NEW PROVING GROUND

Our reassignment to the White House brought no regrets. I saw it as new proving ground and was ready to face anything. The doubts I had when I first joined the Vice President's team were not there this time around. I was surprisingly calm and rather confident to perform my new assignment at the White House, because I carried the knowledge and experiences passed on to me by my mentors. I was reporting to the White House, not only as newly made Senior Chief Ariel P. De Guzman but also as Elias Rodriguez, Herman Capati, Romeo Cruz, Rudy Arca, Florencio Chan, Angel Paraoan, and Orlando Frilles—all in one. Unknown to them, I represented all of them.

We found the White House job assignments, as expected, all filled. No vacancies. It was a tough situation for Orlando and me. We became two extra hands every place we thought we could be of service. Upon learning the situation, the President took us on as his Personal Stewards. Orlando and I had to take turns working every other day on rotation. We were not assigned to work in the White House Mess. Instead, we worked at the White House Mansion and occasionally in the Oval Office to help the civilian Oval Office Steward, Domingo Quicho.

Our main responsibilities at the time were to ensure the President's wardrobe and personal items were always readily available. When we traveled with him throughout America and around the world, our jobs were to ensure the President and First Lady's comfort from the moment they arrived at their hotel suite to the moment they departed for the next event location. Orlando and I played leapfrog with our assignments. While I took care of the President and the First Lady at one site, Orlando prepared to receive them at the next destination. We used every means of transportation to be at least one day or so ahead of the President. We flew ahead with the White House communication plane, secret service car plane, or whatever White House transportation could provide for us. If space was available, Orlando and I flew home with the President onboard Air Force One.

Keeping up with President Bush's many trips was challenging. His constant travel plans led us to take on another Mess Management Specialist/Personal Steward, Richard Sanvictores. His additional assistance was a relief.

Since presidential chefs handled all food preparation at the White House, my culinary involvement took place on events held away from the White House. Camp David and Walker's Point in Kennebunkport, Maine, were two places of my showmanship during those years. Camp David is an extension of the White House in entertaining foreign dignitaries, heads of state, cabinet members, friends, and relatives. Whenever there was a presidential retreat at Camp David, it gave me the chance to perform and show my skills catering to all of them. Working together with the Camp's own Mess Management Specialist, I always had abundant help.

SAYING GOOD-BYE

In January of 1993, while President and Mrs. Bush prepared their final departure from the White House, I flew to Houston, Texas, to help open up their temporary residence. Jack and Bobbie Fitch, lifelong friends of the Bush family, offered their former home while the Bushes' new house was being built in the same neighborhood. I flew back to Washington, D.C., once the Houston residence was in move-in condition. My last assignment for the outgoing President and Mrs. Bush was to sneak Millie and Ranger

The Office of the White House Mess prints this on its daily menu, which explains its unique history.

THE WHITE HOUSE MESS HISTORY

Navy Stewards were first utilized to provide food service to the Commander in Chief as far back as 1880 aboard the Presidential Yacht USS *Dispatch*, while President Rutherford B. Hayes was in office. Since that time, the Navy has assigned their best Stewardsman to the White House to prepare the finest foods and provide outstanding food service for the President around the world.

In 1942, President Franklin D. Roosevelt established the presidential retreat tucked away in the Catoctin Mountains and named it Shangri-la (renamed Camp David by President Dwight D. Eisenhower in 1953 in honor of his grandson David).

President Roosevelt directed the Navy to provide messing services at Shangri-la and that Navy Stewards from the presidential yacht *The Sequoia* should operate the facility. This established the precedent for Navy personnel to serve the President and his staff ashore.

In 1951, while President Harry S. Truman was in office, Rear Admiral Robert L. Dennison, Naval Aide to the President, recommended a Commissioned Officers' Mess to be established at the White House. On June 11, 1951, the White House Mess was established under the guidance of Lieutenant Commander Leo W. Roberts, Supply Corps, USN, and Presidential Mess Officer aboard the USS *Williamsburg*. The White House Mess remains located on the ground floor of the West Wing. Following several decades of naval tradition and pride in direct support to our nation's president, the Mess functions much the same way it did in its earlier days.

During its prestigious history, the men and women of the White House Mess have received the Joint Meritorious Unit Award with one oak-leaf cluster, the Navy Unit Commendation and the Meritorious Unit Commendation for continuous outstanding performance in direct support of the President of the United States.

out in my Toyota pickup through the White House south lawn western gate. I was trying to dodge curious onlookers and all the press cameras. Ranger, disturbed by all the
commotion, stood up and was spotted by a reporter who pointed at us. We were filmed
driving away. The news clip that ran that day was titled, "As the Clintons are moving
in, the Bushes are sneaking out." The article pictured two huge rigs on the south lawn,
perhaps filled with the Clintons' household effects being unloaded. The other news clip
was of a stone-faced pickup driver (yours truly) and Ranger staring straight ahead.

I took Millie and Ranger directly to Andrews Air Force Base Terminal. With the
dogs as my pass, the military guards waved me through the hangar, and I parked far
away from thousands of well-wishers awaiting the Bushes' arrival from the White
House. The jumbo plane was filled with staff members, including the outgoing administration, relatives, and friends accompanying the President and Mrs. Bush to Houston.
All planned to see them off the plane in Houston and return to Washington, D.C.

I was assigned to take the dogs aboard Air Force One and turn them over to the
flight stewards, but I decided to hang on to those two dogs for as long as I could. All

Every weekday morning before 7:00 A.M. President Bush would pass through the south lawn of the White House to give the dogs a short exercise before heading toward the Oval Office. But he kept the dogs in the Oval Office as much as he could. President Reagan, during his tenure, would bring back assorted nuts to the White House from his weekend retreats at Camp David. He then fed the squirrels in the Rose Garden on weekdays, as he often had lunch outdoors. President Bush, the nation's Vice President at the time, lunched with President Reagan every Wednesday of the week, and he'd watch as the President fed the squirrels. When President Bush took office, he didn't want to endanger the White House squirrel population by letting Ranger and Millie run loose. Ranger would stand vigilant by the Oval Office window, on the lookout for small animal movements, while Millie settled in to sleep by the President's Oval Office table. On the way to my workplaces at the White House residence (third and fourth floors), I always swung by the Oval Office to receive the plan of the day, and Ranger anxiously waited for me and then tagged along to the residence, with Millie leisurely following behind. I often wondered whether it was me they loved to see or just the idea of being outdoors again to chase more squirrels.

Millie loved to run toward Marine One as it landed on the south lawn. I'd have to hold her back until the Marine guard opened the door of the helicopter. Millie knew that out of that door would come the President and Mrs. Bush from a trip. She'd make a beeline for Marine One, wagging her almost nonexistent tail, while Ranger ran around the compound chasing anything that moved, completely oblivious to the arriving party.

the well-wishers were looking toward the horizon, anxiously awaiting the arrival of the Marine One helicopter. No one paid any attention to my pickup. No one saw the dogs with their heads on my lap, asleep, while I scratched their ears and heads. And no one saw me openly crying either. I would not only miss the Bush family, but I would also miss those two dogs, or as Mrs. Bush sometimes called them, Millie De Guzman and Ranger De Guzman.

The dogs were attached to me; I immensely grieved their departure. When Marine One hovered over the landing zone, I walked the dogs toward Air Force One. As the President and Mrs. Bush shook hands with the Air Force One ground crew, the dogs ran up the stairs. I simply handed their leashes to President Bush. We said our good-byes, and they told me to keep in touch. Those were their last words to me and the last time we would ever see each other—so I thought.

BACK TO BASICS IN FLORIDA

I left the White House in April 1993 and transferred to Pensacola, Florida, with my family. It was great to be back to the regular Navy, but the regular Navy life I was accustomed to had evolved. New computers and advanced technology were implemented by the time I returned. Young, talented sailors who were professionally trained by the U.S. Navy surrounded me. They made my transition easy, and I fit in quickly. I was assigned Leading Master Chief Mess Management Specialist at the Enlisted Dining Facility at Corry Station in Pensacola, Florida. The facility catered and served more than three thousand meals daily to students and instructors at the Naval Training Center. I supervised more than ninety Mess Management Specialists and other military and civilian food service personnel. I was also designated Food Service Officer, which is a title normally assigned to a Commissioned Officer.

ONE OF MY LOVES LOST

One day, I received a call from a familiar voice. It was Mr. Bush informing me that Ranger was put to sleep. It was a sad day for everyone. Ranger suffered bone cancer or something. I remember saying, "Thank you, sir," for getting the news to me.

I loved that dog as if he were my very own. Ranger slept in my cabin each time I went to Camp David. Whenever I was on duty, the dog was always within five feet of me at the White House mansion. I remember how I painstakingly brushed his tangled ears after he romped around in the woods, and how the two dogs rode with me to Camp David. I remember the day Mr. Bush asked me to go bass fishing at a private pond at Catoctin Mountain and help keep an eye on Ranger. Mr. Bush feared that Ranger might take off after animals he spotted in the woods and get lost. Instead, I remember Ranger diving in the pond trying to catch the largemouth bass the President hooked! I also remember the facial expressions of the Secret Service agents who knew Ranger, soaking wet and covered with foul mud, would jump in one of their vehicles at any given moment.

I remember the time I took Doro, Mr. and Mrs. Bush's youngest daughter, and the two dogs to Andrews Air Force Base in Maryland to meet the First Lady's plane. Mrs. Bush was on her way from an out-of-town event to pick up Doro and the dogs before heading to Maine. Their plane was delayed, so I sat on an outdoor bench and took the dog leashes off for relief. The two dogs quietly sat by me until Ranger spotted a hare. He took off, in full speed, after the hare and quickly caught it. He carried the hare by the neck and dropped it in front of me. Proudly he looked up, expecting a reward. The hare groggily stood up and with wobbly hind legs hopped away from Ranger, attempting to escape. Millie, in one bound, landed on the hare's back, grabbed it by the neck, and in two quick sideways swings finished the job. She then dropped the hare and glanced at Ranger as if saying, "That's how you do it, son." I miss Ranger.

A SUMMER OF CHANGE

I had another phone conversation with Mr. Bush in the spring of 1994. This time, he asked if I could break away from my military duty and head to Maine to provide temporary help for the summer. I immediately agreed. I thought it would be very nice to serve and be with them again. Then a lightbulb clicked on over my head and I thought, Why should it only be on a temporary basis and not a permanent one? I wrote to them and asked, "I decided to retire from active military duty, could they use my services?" They quickly responded that they both wanted to discuss it with me. I traveled from Pensacola to Houston to meet with them.

The meeting became an interview for the job as their Chef/House Manager. I arrived at their place in Houston on a Sunday just as they were returning from church. The gate opened and a Secret Service agent allowed me in. Millie must have been looking out the window from inside the house, because when Mrs. Bush opened the

A happy photo op to signify the end of the President's summer visit to Walker's Point. Shown from left to right: Mrs. Barbara Bush, President George W. Bush, me, Marvin Bush, and Doro Koch.

door, Millie trotted toward me, ignoring everyone else and wiggling her cutoff tail. She remembered me all right. I love that dog.

In the summer of 1994, I took a month's vacation from my military duty and went to Walker's Point. I took over the kitchen, relieving Paula, who had performed the job since April. The summer of 1993, according to Paula, was the worst summer she ever experienced. It was the first summer after President Bush left the White House. Paula had no one to assist her. No presidential logistic support and no more help from Orlando or me. Paula was all by herself to do everything and, at the time, she was seventy-five years old! She was so glad I came to help even only for a month that summer.

FROM MILITARY TO CIVILIAN LIFE

In December 1994, I retired from the U.S. Navy and headed to Houston with my family to become Texas residents. My family braced for the transition and uncertainties of civilian life. After twenty-five years in the military, it took time to adjust to the

It's become a traditional annual event for the household staff to be invited to an annual Christmas party at the Vice President's House with the Bush family. This picture was taken in 1982 during the early years of Mr. Bush's tenure. Next to me are my beautiful wife, Elizabeth, and my youngest son, Orville, who was only one week old when I first began to work at the Vice President's House in October 1981.

Standing next to Vice President Bush was the Official Photographer of the U.S. Vice President, Cynthia Johnson; next to her was Elias Rodriguez, who made the final decision in making me the seventh member of the military staff at the Vice President's House.

change of environment. From Houston, the nearest military installation is in San Antonio, Texas, a three-hour drive. (A military base is where servicemen and their families find solace and enjoy the services and benefits it provides.) Although Houston doesn't have a fully active military base, it's a great city to live in. Everything is abundantly available. My wife and I love to cook our own meals, but we also enjoy savoring someone else's toil, and Houston is the right place to sample all kinds of cuisine.

I enjoy Houston for seven months out of the year. I spend the remaining five months working in Kennebunkport, Maine, since President and Mrs. Bush spend their summers there. I usually travel as early as a week ahead of them to open the Walker's Point compound, a beautiful 11.9-acre property.

The summers at Walker's Point are my busy season. Sons and daughters, in-laws and grandchildren, occupy all the bedrooms at various times during the summer. With the help of Paula and other recruits, I prepare three meals a day, seven days a week. Grandchildren receive different menus from adults and are served at separate hours. I serve vegetarian menus, non-dairy meals, boxed lunches for beachgoers, meals-to-go for the avid boat riders and fishermen, tea for visiting guests, cocktails before dinner, occasional formal receptions, cookouts, meetings, clambakes, birthday celebrations, swimming pool parties, and any last-minute events. I also prepare for the arrival of dignitaries, heads of state, or high officials from across the globe. But no matter how busy my summers get, the thrill I experienced walking into this job is the thrill I receive today. I love my work.

APPETIZERS

Crudités with Curry Dip • Clam Dip • Avocado Dip • Doro's Tex-Mex Dip • Mushroom Croustades • Caviar Croustades • Shrimp and Blue Cheese Croustades • Cheese Cups • Scallion-Cheese Squares • Pastry-Wrapped Brie with Almonds • Pastry-Wrapped Pineapple Cream Cheese • Chinese Egg Rolls • Beth's Philippine Lumpia • Empanadas • Crab Puffs • Cheese Puff Delights • Mushroom Quiches • Sausage Cheese Balls • Bologna Roll

Doro's Tex–Mex Dip

Crudités with Curry Dip

If fresh pineapple is in season when I make this appetizer, I'll carve out one ripe pineapple in the shape of a Labuyo or Sarimanok rooster (see page 82) and fill the hollowed shell with dip. Place the rooster cup in the center or on one end of a tray filled with ornately arranged raw vegetables.

FOR DIP

2 cups mayonnaise
4 teaspoons curry powder
4 teaspoons ketchup
2 teaspoons lemon juice
4 teaspoons honey
4 teaspoons grated onion
4 teaspoons cognac or brandy
1 teaspoon Tabasco sauce
Salt

FOR CRUDITÉS

Red bell peppers
Green bell peppers
Cucumbers
Celery stalks
Carrots
Cauliflower
Broccoli
Cherry tomatoes
Red radishes
Pitted jumbo black olives

For dip: In a large bowl, combine mayonnaise, curry powder, ketchup, lemon juice, honey, onion, cognac, and Tabasco. Season with pinch of salt and mix well. Cover and chill. Transfer to a serving fruit cup or bowl just before serving time.

For a less spicy dip, add additional ¼ cup mayonnaise instead of decreasing Tabasco sauce to retain its taste.

For crudités: Uniformly slice and cut bell peppers, cucumbers, celery, and carrots into sticks. Cut off stems of cauliflower and broccoli; separate into bite-sized florets. Wash and pat dry cherry tomatoes. Elaborately carve radishes, discarding stems and roots. Drain black olives and pat dry. Arrange crudités in neat rows around tray using the colors to dictate presentation. Leave a space in the center or on one side of the tray to accommodate the hollowed-out fruit cup or bowl filled with dip.

Makes about 2½ cups dip

Clam Dip

This is equally delicious made with crab.

> 1 (6½-ounce) can minced clams or crab
> 8 ounces cream cheese, at room temperature
> 2 tablespoons minced shallot
> 1 tablespoon Worcestershire sauce
> 2 teaspoons dry sherry
> 1 teaspoon hot sauce
> Salt and pepper
> Corn chip scoops or crackers, for serving

Heat oven to 350º.

In a large bowl, mix together the clams, cream cheese, shallot, Worcestershire, sherry, and hot sauce. Season with salt and pepper.

Transfer to 8-inch soufflé dish. Bake for 20 minutes, or until bubbly. Transfer to center of a larger serving tray and surround with corn chip scoops or crackers. Serve hot.

Serves 6

Avocado Dip

Use as a dip for Empanadas (page 44) or omit the cilantro and scallion and use as a sauce to complement grilled jumbo shrimp or poached salmon.

> 2 ripe avocados, pitted, peeled, and diced
> 1/3 cup water
> 1/3 cup plus 4 tablespoons heavy cream
> 1/2 teaspoon grated lemon zest
> 3 tablespoons lemon juice
> Salt and pepper
> 1 tablespoon finely chopped cilantro
> 1 tablespoon finely chopped scallion

In food processor fitted with a metal blade, combine avocados, water, 1/3 cup heavy cream, lemon zest and juice, and salt and pepper to taste. Puree until smooth.

Transfer mixture to a small heavy-bottomed saucepan over medium heat and bring to a boil. Reduce heat and simmer gently until sauce reduces to about 1 cup. Remove from heat and fold in 4 tablespoons heavy cream, cilantro, and scallion.

Makes 1 cup

Doro's Tex-Mex Dip

Dorothy Koch, youngest daughter of the President and Mrs. Bush, proudly shared this recipe with me. I serve this dip with chips during patio or poolside barbecue events and during the annual picnic attended by the U.S. Secret Service Bush Protective Division and their families at Walker's Point.

7 scallions, chopped
2 medium tomatoes, diced
1½ cups shredded lettuce
1 cup shredded sharp Cheddar cheese
1 (10½-ounce) can ripe pitted olives, drained and chopped
1 cup chunky Picante sauce (mild or hot)
1 (12½-ounce) can chili (no beans)
1 cup guacamole, or 2 ripe avocados, seeded, peeled, and diced
1 (14½-ounce) can refried beans
1 cup sour cream
Cilantro sprigs, stems removed
Lemon or lime wedges (optional)
Corn chip scoops or tortilla chips, for serving

In a large bowl, combine three-quarters of the scallions, tomatoes, lettuce, cheese, and olives. Add Picante sauce, chili, guacamole, refried beans, and sour cream. Blend mixture gently.

Transfer dip to one large or two smaller serving bowls. Level top. Garnish with remaining scallions, tomatoes, lettuce, cheese, and olives in colorful rows arranged on top of the dip.

Garnish edges with sprigs of cilantro and lime or lemon wedges to squeeze over dip, if desired.

Surround dip with baskets or smaller containers filled with your favorite store-bought corn chips or tortilla chips.

Serves 24

This was taken during the 2004 summer picnic. As I'm busy grilling hamburgers and hot dogs, the one-man transportation committee takes the wheel and transports naive passengers, such as little Andrew Almblad (son of a Secret Service agent), in circles around the compound. Heedless of posted "Keep Off the Grass" signs, he always manages to send the go-cart careening off the road.

During the end of each summer in Maine, a picnic is held at the Walker's Point compound. (The only "end of summer picnic" that was canceled was after 9-11.)

The picnic is attended by U.S. Secret Service agents assigned to the Bush Protective Division and their families and the Special Officers Division assigned to Walker's Point and their families.

Our favorite picnic area is near the grounds adjacent to the swimming pool, where children can swim under close adult supervision. The pool is a short walking distance from the dock, where agents take turns providing guests with rides around the cove on their rubber speed craft and the President's boat, *Fidelity (I, II,* and *III).*

Doro's Tex-Mex Dip is a crowd favorite at this picnic. Hamburgers and hot dogs are, of course, the main offerings. Assorted fresh fruit and Klondike Bars are offered for desserts.

Mushroom Croustades

4 tablespoons unsalted butter
3 tablespoons finely chopped shallot
½ pound mushrooms, coarsely chopped
2 tablespoons all-purpose flour
1 cup heavy cream
½ teaspoon salt
⅛ teaspoon cayenne pepper
1 tablespoon chopped parsley
1½ tablespoons chopped chives
1 teaspoon fresh lemon juice
24 croustades (page 34)
4 tablespoons grated Parmesan cheese

Heat oven to 350º.

In a medium skillet over medium heat, melt butter. Add shallot and cook for about 4 minutes, until softened, stirring frequently to avoid browning. Stir in mushrooms and cook until all moisture has evaporated, 10–15 minutes.

Remove from heat; add flour and stir to coat mixture. Add cream. Return to heat and cook, stirring until thickened and bubbly. Remove from heat; stir in salt, cayenne pepper, parsley, chives, and lemon juice.

Pour into a bowl and allow mixture to cool.

Fill croustades with mushroom filling, mounding slightly. Sprinkle each croustade with ½ teaspoon Parmesan cheese. Place on ungreased cookie sheet. Bake for 10 minutes and then finish under broiler briefly.

Makes 24 croustades

Croustades (Toast Cups)

Heat oven to 350º. Coat mini-muffin tins (1¾-inch) lightly with pan spray.

Use a 2½-inch biscuit cutter to cut rounds from very thin slices of white bread (I use Pepperidge Farm). Gently press bread into muffin tins, creating cups. Bake for 10–15 minutes, until crisp and golden brown around edges. Lift out of muffin tins and cool completely on wire racks.

You can make these a day in advance and store in an airtight container.

Caviar Croustades

> 4 ounces cream cheese, softened
> ⅓ cup sour cream
> 3 tablespoons mayonnaise
> 1 large egg, hard-cooked
> 1 scallion, finely chopped
> Lemon pepper
> 24 croustades (recipe above)
> 4.4 ounces Beluga caviar (or your favorite)
> Lemon arrowheads (see Note)

In a bowl, combine and beat cream cheese and sour cream until smooth. Stir in mayonnaise. Separate white from yolk of egg and mash white (save yolk for another use). Add egg whites, scallion, and lemon pepper to taste. Stir well.

Fill croustades with mayonnaise–cream cheese mixture and top with 1 teaspoon caviar. Top each caviar mound with a lemon arrowhead.

Makes 24 croustades

Note: To make arrowheads, cut a lemon into thin slices. Cut away the rind and discard seeds. Cut each round into 8 wedges. Each will resemble the shape of an arrowhead.

Shrimp and Blue Cheese Croustades

60 small (71/90) frozen shrimp, defrosted
60 croustades (page 34)
6 tablespoons mayonnaise
6 ounces Saga blue cheese (or other
creamy blue cheese)
Grated Parmesan cheese
4 sprigs fresh rosemary, stems removed,
leaves chopped finely
Chopped parsley

Bring large saucepan of water to a boil. Add shrimp and blanch until just heated through, about 25 seconds. Drain and allow to cool to room temperature.

Position oven rack 4 inches from heat source. Heat broiler.

Place 1 shrimp in each croustade. In a small bowl, blend together mayonnaise and blue cheese. Add a teaspoonful to each croustade. Sprinkle with Parmesan cheese and rosemary. Place croustades on baking sheet.

Broil until cheese melts and shrimp are heated through, about 1 minute. Transfer to platter. Garnish croustades with parsley.

Makes 28 croustades

Cheese Cups

8 ounces cream cheese, softened
1 cup crumbled feta cheese
1 teaspoon salt
1 teaspoon ground pepper
1 large egg, lightly beaten
90 frozen phyllo cups (6 packages;
     available in many grocery stores)
30 pimiento-stuffed olives, sliced
Dried dill, for garnish

Heat oven to 350º. Lightly grease 2 baking sheets. In a small bowl, mix cream cheese, feta cheese, salt, and pepper. Add egg and mix well.

Place 1 teaspoon of cheese filling in each phyllo cup.

Place cups on baking sheets. Bake for 8–12 minutes, until golden brown. Top each with a stuffed olive ring and dill.

Makes 90 cheese cups

Scallion-Cheese Squares

2 tablespoons unsalted butter
2 bunches scallions, chopped
3 tablespoons chopped parsley
6 large eggs
¼ cup sour cream
½ cup soft bread crumbs (see Note)
¾ cup grated Swiss cheese
½ cup Parmesan cheese

Heat oven to 350°. Butter a 9-inch square baking pan.

In a saucepan over medium heat, melt butter. Add scallions and cook until soft. Remove from heat; add parsley and set aside.

In a bowl, beat eggs well. Add sour cream, bread crumbs, Swiss cheese, and ¼ cup Parmesan cheese. Stir in scallion-parsley mixture. Mix well.

Pour into baking pan. Sprinkle top with remaining ¼ cup Parmesan cheese. Bake 10 minutes. Cut into 16 squares and serve hot.

Makes 16 squares

Note: To make soft bread crumbs, cut crusts from slices of close-textured white bread. Cut bread in pieces and pulse in food processor to make crumbs. One slice of bread will make about ½ cup crumbs.

Pastry-Wrapped Brie with Almonds

FOR PASTRY

¾ cup all-purpose flour
4 tablespoons unsalted butter, softened
4 ounces cream cheese, softened

FOR FILLING

1 (8-ounce) round Brie
4 tablespoons slivered almonds

1 large egg beaten with 1 teaspoon water,
    for egg wash
Sliced apples (tossed with lemon juice)
    and assorted crackers, for serving

For pastry: In a large bowl, combine flour, butter, and cream cheese. Beat with electric mixer at low speed, scraping sides often, until dough forms, 2–3 minutes. Shape into a ball and wrap with plastic. Chill for at least 30 minutes in refrigerator.

Heat oven to 350º.

Divide dough in half. On lightly floured surface, roll each half to ⅛ inch thick. Cut a 7-inch circle from each half. Place one circle on cookie sheet.

For filling: With a sharp knife, cut off rind from top of Brie and place Brie in center of pastry circle.

In a small dry frying pan over medium heat, stir slivered almonds constantly with wooden spoon until lightly browned. Remove pan from heat and while still warm, spread toasted almonds evenly on top of Brie.

Top Brie and almonds with second pastry circle, pressing down on top of Brie to hold almonds in place. Pinch edges to seal. Flute edges as desired. Decorate top using pastry cutouts shaped into grape clusters, grape leaves, and vines. Brush top and sides of pastry with egg wash.

Bake for 15–20 minutes, or until golden brown. Remove from cookie sheet immediately. Let stand 30 minutes to allow cheese to set. Serve with apple slices and assorted crackers.

Serves 8

Pastry-Wrapped Pineapple Cream Cheese

FOR PASTRY

¾ cup all-purpose flour
4 tablespoons unsalted butter, softened
4 ounces cream cheese, softened

FOR FILLING

6 tablespoons crushed pineapple, drained
8 ounces cream cheese, softened

1 egg yolk, beaten
Assorted crackers and sliced apples (tossed with lemon juice), for serving

For pastry: In a large bowl, combine flour, butter, and cream cheese. Beat with electric mixer at low speed, scraping sides often, until dough forms, 2–3 minutes. Shape into a ball. Wrap with plastic and chill for at least 30 minutes in refrigerator.

Heat oven to 350°. Place dough between two sheets of wax paper and roll into a 12 x 4-inch rectangle.

For filling: Spread 3 tablespoons crushed pineapple in center of dough. Place cream cheese on pineapple; top cream cheese with remaining 3 tablespoons crushed pineapple. Allow pineapple to drip down sides of cream cheese.

Enclose cream cheese with dough by bringing sides of dough together and pressing edges to seal cream cheese and pineapple completely. Trim edges and use trimmings to decorate top of pastry.

Place on lightly greased cookie sheet. Brush pastry with egg yolk. Bake for 15–18 minutes, or until lightly browned. Serve warm with assorted crackers and apple slices.

Serves 6–8

Chinese Egg Rolls

FOR MARINADE

1 teaspoon dry sherry
1 teaspoon cornstarch
¼ teaspoon salt
⅓ pound finely ground pork

FOR FILLING

4 dried shiitake mushrooms
2 cups hot water
4 cups shredded cabbage
½ cup shredded carrots
6 tablespoons vegetable oil
½ cup shredded bamboo shoots
1 teaspoon salt
¼ teaspoon pepper
1½ teaspoons sugar
3 tablespoons soy sauce
3 tablespoons cornstarch
¼ cup chunky peanut butter
1 tablespoon sesame oil

FOR ASSEMBLY

1 egg white
2 tablespoons cold water
12 (8-inch) egg roll skins (available
in many grocery stores)
6 cups vegetable oil

For marinade: Combine sherry, cornstarch, and salt in a medium bowl. Add ground pork and stir to mix well. Set aside to marinate for at least 20 minutes.

For filling: Meanwhile, in another bowl, soak mushrooms in hot water until soft, about 20 minutes. Drain and remove hard stems. Chop mushroom caps and set aside.

Bring a large saucepan of water to a boil over high heat. Add cabbage and carrots and cook for 2 minutes. Drain and rinse under cold running water. Drain again and squeeze out excess water. Return vegetables to saucepan and set aside.

In a wok over medium-high heat, heat vegetable oil. When oil starts to smoke, add marinated pork and stir-fry for 2 minutes. Remove pork with slotted spoon, leaving oil in wok, and transfer to a bowl. Set aside.

In the same wok, combine mushrooms and bamboo shoots and stir-fry until soft, about 1 minute.

Add cabbage and carrots and continue stir-frying for another minute. Add cooked pork to stir-fried vegetables and mix well. Stir in salt, pepper, sugar, soy sauce, and cornstarch. Remove from heat and stir in peanut butter and sesame oil. Transfer to a large bowl. Allow mixture to cool to room temperature. Refrigerate until ready to assemble.

For assembly: In a small bowl, beat egg white and water until frothy to use as paste.

Stir filling just before you add it to wrappers. This will allow all liquids to coat filling evenly and not settle in the bottom of the bowl.

Place 1 egg roll skin on a flat surface with corners at the top and bottom, left and right. Spoon ⅓ cup filling just below the center of egg roll skin. Fold bottom corner up over filling. Roll once and fold left and right corners over filling. Continue rolling toward top corner. Dab egg-water paste under the top corner. Press firmly to seal. Repeat with remaining egg roll skins and filling.

In a wok over medium-high heat, heat oil to 350°. Carefully lower in 4 egg rolls with a slotted spoon. Deep-fry for 2 minutes, until bottom is golden brown. Turn each egg roll and fry other side for 2 minutes more, until golden brown.

Remove with a slotted spoon. Transfer fried egg rolls into deep pan, lined heavily with paper towels; stand on ends to drain excess oil. Repeat frying process with remaining egg rolls.

Makes 12 egg rolls

Beth's Philippine Lumpia

This is my wife Elizabeth's version of Philippine egg rolls, which she considers her pride-and-joy recipe. I often cut them in half to serve as appetizers. Three whole pieces are an ample side dish served with dipping sauces.

FOR FILLING

1/2 pound lean ground beef
1/2 pound lean ground pork
2 tablespoons soy sauce
2 large eggs, beaten
2 celery stalks, chopped
1 carrot, chopped
1 small onion, chopped
1/2 cup frozen peas, defrosted
1/2 cup frozen corn, defrosted
4 garlic cloves, minced
1 teaspoon salt
1/2 teaspoon pepper
1/2 cup golden raisins (optional)

FOR ASSEMBLY

1 egg white
2 tablespoons cold water
25 frozen egg roll wrappers
     (also known as Lumpia wrappers),
      defrosted (available in specialty markets)
2 cups cooking oil

For filling: In a large bowl, combine ground meats, soy sauce, eggs, celery, carrot, onion, peas, corn, garlic, salt, pepper, and raisins, if desired. Mix well. Let mixture marinate for at least 30 minutes in refrigerator.

For assembly: In a small bowl, beat egg white and water until frothy to use as paste. Unwrap wrappers and keep covered with damp paper towels to prevent drying.

Place 1 round egg roll wrapper on a flat surface or large dinner plate. Place 4 teaspoonfuls filling 1 inch from the bottom edge of wrapper. Shape filling into cylinder 4 inches long. Fold bottom edge over filling. Roll once tightly toward center; fold in left and right edges toward center. Continue rolling. Dab paste under the top edge. Press firmly to seal. Lumpia should be about 4 inches long and ¾–1 inch in diameter. For eye appeal and best presentation, keep size consistent.

Repeat with remaining wrappers and filling. Stack 12 egg rolls together in 2 layers. Wrap with wax paper and freeze at least 3 hours or overnight before frying.

In a frying pan over medium heat, heat oil. Carefully lower 6 lumpia into oil using tongs. Fry for 2 minutes on one side. Turn lumpia and fry other side for 2 minutes more, or until all sides are evenly golden brown. Remove with tongs and transfer to deep pan lined heavily with paper towels; stand on ends to drain excess oil. Repeat with remaining egg rolls.

Makes 25 lumpia

Empanadas

FOR PASTRY

8 ounces cream cheese, softened
8 tablespoons (1 stick) unsalted butter, softened
1½ cups all-purpose flour

FOR FILLING

½ pound ground beef or turkey
1 teaspoon ground cumin
½ teaspoon cayenne pepper
½ teaspoon salt
¼ teaspoon pepper
½ cup canned corn, drained
Half of 1 (15-ounce) can red kidney beans, mashed
2 tablespoons chopped scallion
1 egg white
2 tablespoons water
1 egg, beaten

Avocado Dip (page 30), for serving

For pastry: In a large bowl, mix together cheese, butter, and flour until soft and pliable. Wrap in plastic and chill for at least 30 minutes.

For filling: In a skillet over medium-high heat, brown ground beef. Drain in colander and return to skillet. Season with cumin, cayenne pepper, salt, and pepper. Mix in corn and kidney beans until well incorporated. Remove from heat, stir in scallion, and allow to cool.

Heat oven to 350º.

In a small bowl, beat egg white with water to use as paste.

Dust working surface with flour and roll pastry into a ⅛-inch-thick rectangle.

Using a 2-inch biscuit cutter, cut rounds of pastry. Place 1 heaping teaspoon filling in center of each pastry circle. Brush edge with paste. Fold circle in half to form half-moon. Seal edge with fork. Transfer empanadas to baking sheets.

Brush tops with beaten egg. Bake for 10–12 minutes, or until golden brown.

Serve Empanadas with Avocado Dip.

Makes about 60 empanadas

Note: Once cooked, empanadas may be frozen for as long as 6 months. Store in airtight container or sealable plastic bags. When ready to use, defrost and microwave 1 minute.

Crab Puffs

$\frac{1}{2}$ *cup grated sharp Cheddar cheese*
3 scallions, finely chopped
1 teaspoon Worcestershire sauce
1 teaspoon dry mustard
1 (6$\frac{1}{2}$-ounce) can crabmeat, drained
      and picked over
1 cup water
8 tablespoons (1 stick) unsalted butter,
      cut into pieces
$\frac{1}{4}$ *teaspoon salt*
1 cup all-purpose flour
4 large eggs

Heat oven to 400°.

In a medium bowl, combine cheese, scallions, Worcestershire, mustard, and crabmeat. Mix well and set aside.

In a large saucepan, combine water, butter, and salt and bring to a boil. When butter is melted, add flour and beat until mixture leaves side of pan and forms a ball. Transfer to a mixing bowl. Add in eggs, one at a time, beating well with an electric mixer or wooden spoon after each addition. Stir in crab mixture.

Transfer mixture into a pastry bag fitted with large star tip and pipe teaspoon-sized mounds onto ungreased baking sheet. Bake for 15 minutes. Reduce heat to 350º. Bake for 10 more minutes.

Makes about 4 dozen puffs

Cheese Puff Delights

12 very thin slices whole wheat or white bread (I use Pepperidge Farm Very Thin)
1 cup grated sharp Cheddar cheese
½ onion, grated
¼ cup mayonnaise
1 tablespoon Worcestershire sauce
¼ teaspoon salt
⅛ teaspoon black pepper
Hot sauce (optional)

Heat oven to 350º.

With a 1½-inch biscuit cutter, cut 2 rounds from each slice of bread. Arrange rounds on baking sheet and bake for 4 minutes. Turn rounds over and bake another 4 minutes, or until both sides of bread are no longer soft to the touch and are slightly brown in color. Cool on rack.

In a bowl, mix together cheese, onion, mayonnaise, Worcestershire, salt, and pepper until well blended. Add hot sauce, if desired.

Position oven rack in middle of oven and heat broiler.

Mound cheese on toast rounds. Arrange on baking sheet 1 inch apart from each other.

Broil just until tops begin to melt. Watch broiling process closely; do not allow cheese mixture to melt and ooze away from bread rounds. Serve immediately.

Makes 24 puffs

Mushroom Quiches

4 tablespoons unsalted butter
1 garlic clove, minced
1½ pounds mushrooms, chopped
4 scallions, chopped
2 teaspoons chopped fresh oregano
2 teaspoons chopped fresh basil
1 teaspoon salt
½ teaspoon pepper
½ teaspoon dried marjoram
½ teaspoon dried thyme
½ teaspoon dry mustard
4 eggs, beaten
¾ cup heavy cream
Juice and grated zest of ½ lemon
1 (64-count) party cups (available in many grocery stores)

FOR TOPPING

½ cup mayonnaise
2 tablespoons heavy cream
1 tablespoon dried dill weed, crushed

Position oven rack in lower third of oven and heat to 375º. Coat a sheet pan lightly with pan spray.

In a large skillet over medium-high heat, melt unsalted butter. Add garlic, mushrooms, and scallions and cook, stirring constantly, until all liquid has evaporated, 10–12 minutes. Stir in oregano, basil, salt, pepper, marjoram, thyme, and mustard. Cook for 2 more minutes. Remove from heat and allow mixture to cool.

In a large bowl, combine eggs, cream, and lemon juice and zest and beat well. Add mushrooms and fold into custard.

Arrange party cups in rows on sheet pan, barely touching each other. Fill each cup three-quarters full with mushroom-custard mixture. Bake filled cups for 2 minutes, or until slightly firm.

Remove partially baked quiches from oven and allow to cool while preparing topping.

Heat broiler.

For topping: In a small bowl, combine mayonnaise, heavy cream, and dill weed.

Dab ½ teaspoon topping onto each quiche; level with knife to fill up to rim of each cup. Place sheet pan under broiler for 1 minute, or until topping starts to bubble and brown slightly. Serve immediately.

Makes 64 quiches

Sausage Cheese Balls

2 pounds uncooked bulk sausage, crumbled
1½ cups Bisquick
4 cups grated sharp Cheddar cheese
½ cup finely chopped onion
½ cup finely diced celery
½ teaspoon garlic powder
¼ teaspoon salt
Dash of ground pepper
Dash of hot pepper flakes
Rich Mornay Sauce (page 200) for serving

Heat oven to 325º.

In a large bowl, combine sausage, baking mix, cheese, onions, celery, garlic powder, salt, pepper, and hot pepper flakes. Mix well. Form into ¾-inch balls.

Arrange on cookie sheet and bake for 15 minutes, or until golden brown. Serve on toothpicks with Rich Mornay Sauce.

Makes about 6 dozen balls

Bologna Roll

Request an end cut from a bologna sausage from your favorite butcher.

> 3 pounds bologna sausage
> 1 cup Dijon-style mustard
> 2 tablespoons soy sauce
> 1 tablespoon chopped rosemary
> ½ teaspoon finely minced ginger
> 2 tablespoons olive oil
> Assorted crackers, for serving

Heat oven to 425°.

Remove casing from bologna. Cut an X into the rounded end, about 3 inches long and ½ inch deep. Transfer bologna to baking dish lined with aluminum foil.

In a small bowl, combine mustard, soy sauce, rosemary, ginger, and olive oil. Blend well. Spread, covering bologna completely with mustard mixture. Stick 4 toothpicks into slashed sides. Tent toothpicks with another sheet of aluminum foil while being careful not to allow top foil to touch meat and sauce. Allow 2 toothpicks to poke through to permit steam to escape during baking process. Seal edges of foil.

Bake sealed bologna for 15 minutes.

Carve a section of bologna into thin 1½ x 2-inch slices and arrange around bologna roll. Guests may carve more pieces from remaining bologna when presliced pieces are gone. Serve hot with assorted crackers.

Serves 12–16

SOUPS

Iced Cucumber Soup • Frosty Gazpacho • Dottie's Cold Spinach Soup • Artichoke Citrus Soup • Sherry Carrot Soup • Ariel's Onion Soup • Butternut Squash Soup • Tomato Bisque • Texas Tortilla Soup • Curried Zucchini Soup • Walker's Point Clam Chowder • Walker's Point Fish Chowder • Walker's Point Seafood Chowder • Senegalese Soup

Frosty Gazpacho

Iced Cucumber Soup

2 cucumbers, peeled, seeded, and cubed
3 cups chicken broth
2 cups milk
3 white onions, sliced
¼ teaspoon salt
Dash of cayenne pepper
2 tablespoons unsalted butter
¼ cup all-purpose flour
1½ teaspoons chopped fresh dill or fresh mint
1 cup heavy cream or low-fat sour cream
½ cucumber, peeled, seeded, and diced, for garnish
Salt and paprika, for garnish

In a large saucepan over medium-high heat, combine cucumbers, chicken broth, milk, and onions. Bring to a boil and cook until tender.

Remove from heat and puree soup in blender in batches until very smooth. Season with salt and cayenne pepper. Return soup to large saucepan. Set aside.

In a small skillet over low heat, melt butter. Add flour and stir for 2–3 minutes with a wire whisk. Remove pan from heat and add this roux to soup mixture a little at a time, whisking constantly.

Return soup to medium heat and cook, stirring, for 5–6 minutes, until thickened. Stir in dill. Pour into a soup tureen; cover with plastic wrap directly on surface of soup to prevent a skin from forming. Refrigerate at least 6 hours or overnight.

Whisk in heavy cream before serving.

Garnish individual servings with diced cucumber, sprinkled with salt and dashes of paprika. Serve immediately or keep individual bowls of soup refrigerated until ready to serve.

Serves 6

Frosty Gazpacho

2 medium and firm tomatoes, seeded and finely chopped
1 large cucumber, peeled and finely chopped
1 celery stalk, finely chopped
1 small Vidalia or other sweet onion, finely chopped
½ green bell pepper, finely chopped
½ red bell pepper, finely chopped
1½ cups V8 or tomato juice
1 tablespoon light olive oil
2 teaspoons lemon juice
1 teaspoon sugar
1 teaspoon Worcestershire sauce
½ teaspoon hot sauce
2 tablespoons red wine vinegar
2 teaspoons finely chopped parsley
1 small garlic clove, finely chopped
2 teaspoons chopped cilantro
¼ teaspoon salt
Pepper
1 avocado, pitted, peeled, and diced
Sour cream, for serving
Fried sage, for serving (optional; see Note)
Finely chopped basil, for serving
Chopped cilantro, for serving
Lime wedges, for serving

In a large glass bowl, combine tomatoes, cucumber, celery, onion, and bell peppers. Set aside.

In another bowl, combine V8, olive oil, lemon juice, sugar, Worcestershire, hot sauce, red wine vinegar, parsley, minced garlic, cilantro, salt, and pepper to taste.

Combine chopped vegetables with juice mixture. Transfer one-third gazpacho into a separate bowl and freeze mixture for at least 45 minutes before serving time, or until mixture starts to crystallize. Chill remaining mixture in refrigerator until ready to serve, stirring occasionally.

At serving time, fill 6 soup bowls with refrigerated gazpacho. Using ice cream scoop, compactly scoop frozen gazpacho and place in center of chilled soup. Sprinkle diced avocado around frozen mixture. Dab top with sour cream. Top sour cream with fried sage. Sprinkle with chopped basil and cilantro. Garnish each bowl with lime wedges. Serve immediately.

Serves 6

Note: To fry sage, heat 1 inch vegetable oil in a saucepan over medium-high heat to 350º, add sage leaves, and fry for 20 seconds. Turn leaves and fry until crisp, about 5 seconds. Drain on paper towels.

Dottie's Cold Spinach Soup

This is Mrs. Dorothy Walker Bush's—President Bush's mother—special soup.

> 1 (10-ounce) package frozen spinach, defrosted
> 4 cups light cream
> 4 chicken bouillon cubes
> ¼ cup dry vermouth
> ½ teaspoon ground mace
> 1 teaspoon grated lemon zest
> 2 large eggs, hard-cooked and grated or mashed, for serving

In a food processor, puree spinach to a pulp. Set aside.

In a heavy-bottomed saucepan over low heat, scald light cream; do not boil. Add bouillon cubes and stir to dissolve. Add spinach and simmer for 3 minutes.

Remove from heat and stir in vermouth, mace, and lemon zest.

Chill completely before serving and garnish with eggs.

Serves 4

Artichoke Citrus Soup

This recipe is from Jackson Hicks, proprietor of the famous Jackson and Company Catering Services of Houston, Texas. He shared this recipe with me, and it's received overwhelming approval from President and Mrs. Bush and guests on numerous occasions.

4 (13.7-ounce) cans artichoke hearts, drained
4 tablespoons unsalted butter
½ cup minced onion
½ cup finely chopped celery
3 cups chicken broth
4 tablespoons fresh lemon juice
¼ cup cornstarch
3 cups half-and-half
Salt and white pepper
½ cup minced parsley, for garnish
Grated zest of 1 lemon, for garnish

Taste the artichokes. If very salty, rinse well under cool water and drain well. Pull off and discard any tough leaves, then cut the artichoke hearts into quarters. Measure out 2 cups; reserve any leftovers for another use.

In a saucepan over medium heat, melt butter. Add onion and celery and cook, stirring, until vegetables are translucent but not browned. Add broth and half the artichokes and bring to a boil.

In a bowl, combine lemon juice and cornstarch and mix well to eliminate lumps. Add cornstarch mixture to boiling soup in saucepan, stirring with wire whisk. Bring back to a boil and allow soup to boil for 5 minutes.

To finish, add half-and-half and remaining artichoke hearts. Add salt and pepper to taste. Garnish each serving with parsley and lemon zest.

Serves 6

Sherry Carrot Soup

Each year, as soon as I arrive at Walker's Point in May, I prepare this soup and freeze a large quantity (without the cream and sherry) in different-sized containers and label each as such: for 4, 6, 8, or 10 servings.

Serve the soup piping hot or icy cold.

2 tablespoons unsalted butter
1 medium onion, chopped
5 to 6 medium carrots, sliced into ¼-inch rings
½ teaspoon salt
¼ teaspoon ground ginger
¼ teaspoon ground cinnamon
Dash of pepper
3 cups chicken broth
½ cup heavy cream
¼ cup dry sherry

In a large saucepan over medium-high heat, melt butter. Add onion and cook until translucent. Add carrots, salt, ginger, cinnamon, pepper, and chicken broth and bring to a boil. Reduce heat, cover, and simmer until carrots are tender, about 20 minutes.

Process in batches in blender until smooth. Return soup to saucepan. Add heavy cream. Reheat to serving temperature. Taste and correct seasoning, if needed. Stir in sherry.

Serves 4

Ariel's Onion Soup

2 tablespoons unsalted butter
1 tablespoon olive oil
½ pound leeks, white parts only
1 pound shallots, thinly sliced
1 garlic clove, finely chopped
½ teaspoon sugar
3 tablespoons all-purpose flour
8 cups beef broth, heated
4 teaspoons dry vermouth
Dash of Tabasco sauce
Salt and pepper
Cheese toasts, for serving (see Note)

In a heavy saucepan over low heat, heat butter and olive oil. Add leeks, shallots, and garlic and cook for about 15 minutes or until softened, stirring occasionally.

Increase heat to medium-low, add sugar, and cook for about 30 minutes, or until leeks and shallots are golden brown, stirring frequently. Add flour and cook, stirring constantly, for 3 minutes.

Add beef broth, vermouth, and Tabasco; season with salt and pepper. Simmer for 40 minutes.

Divide soup among 8 (8-ounce) crock bowls. Top each with a cheese toast and serve immediately.

Serves 8

Note: For cheese toasts, cut 8 crosswise slices, about ⅓ inch thick, from a loaf of French bread. Place on baking sheet and bake in a preheated 350° oven for 15 minutes, until crisp. Right before serving soup, top each piece of bread with 1 tablespoon grated Gruyère cheese and place under broiler until bubbling and browned in spots.

Butternut Squash Soup

This recipe was shared by Liz Fowler, a longtime friend from Midland, Texas.

    1 (1½–2-pound) butternut squash
    5 cups chicken broth
    ⅓ cup minced onion
    ½ teaspoon salt
    Dash of white pepper
    1 cup sour cream

Peel butternut squash, discard seeds, and cut into 1-inch cubes.

In a large saucepan, bring chicken broth to a boil. Add squash, onion, salt, and pepper and simmer for 25 minutes. Process in batches in blender until smooth.

Return soup to saucepan. Reheat and stir in sour cream.

Serves 8

Tomato Bisque

President Bush loves all kinds of soup. Serve him soup as a first course every day and you will never go wrong. If he asks me to leave a small pot of soup out so he can help himself later, his first choice is this particular recipe.

    2 tablespoons unsalted butter
    ¼ cup chopped carrots
    ½ cup chopped celery
    ½ cup chopped onion
    2½ tablespoons all-purpose flour
    1 (14.5-ounce) can whole plum tomatoes, crushed
    1 teaspoon sugar

½ teaspoon dried marjoram
½ teaspoon dried basil
1 bay leaf
3 cups chicken broth
1 cup heavy cream
½ teaspoon curry powder
⅛ teaspoon white pepper
½ teaspoon paprika
Salt
Dry sherry, for serving
Tabasco sauce, for serving
Grated Parmesan cheese, for serving

In a large heavy-bottomed saucepan over medium-high heat, melt butter. Add carrots, celery, and onion and cook until tender.

Stir in flour and cook, stirring constantly, for 2 minutes. Add canned tomatoes, sugar, marjoram, basil, bay leaf, and chicken broth and simmer for 30 minutes.

Discard bay leaf. Puree soup in batches in blender until smooth. Transfer to double boiler and stir in heavy cream, curry powder, white pepper, paprika, and salt to taste. Simmer until ready to serve.

To serve, offer dry sherry, Tabasco sauce, and grated Parmesan separately. This soup may also be served cold—without the cheese.

Serves 4

Texas Tortilla Soup

8 tablespoons (1 stick) unsalted butter
1 large onion, chopped
1 fresh jalapeño, seeded and chopped
4 garlic cloves, minced
2 large carrots, diced
6 celery stalks, diced
1 pound boneless, skinless chicken (breast or thigh), diced
1 teaspoon ground cumin
1 teaspoon chili powder
1 teaspoon salt
1 teaspoon lemon pepper
½ cup all-purpose flour
1 tablespoon Tabasco sauce
1 (14.5-ounce) can diced tomatoes
5 (14.5-ounce) cans chicken broth
1 cup vegetable oil
4 corn tortillas, cut into strips
1 cup sour cream, for serving
3 avocados, seeded, peeled, and diced, for serving
1 cup grated Parmesan cheese, for serving
Cilantro sprigs, for serving

In a large stockpot over medium-high heat, melt butter. Add onion and cook until translucent. Add jalapeño, garlic, carrots, celery, and chicken and simmer for 5 minutes. Stir in cumin, chili powder, salt, lemon pepper, and flour, and cook, stirring, for a minute or two. Add Tabasco, tomatoes, and chicken broth; simmer for 1 hour.

While soup simmers, heat vegetable oil in a deep skillet. Fry tortilla strips until crisp; drain on paper towels.

To serve, put a few tortilla strips in soup bowls. Fill bowls with soup and top with a spoon each of sour cream, avocado, and grated Parmesan cheese. Garnish with cilantro sprigs.

Serves 10

Curried Zucchini Soup

This recipe is from Mrs. Millie Dent, the wife of Fred Dent, who was President Nixon's Secretary of Commerce. Serve steaming hot with crisp croutons or icy cold with chopped chives. As with the Sherry Carrot Soup, I make huge batches of this soup each month.

> 1 pound zucchini, unpeeled, cut into 1-inch pieces
> 2 tablespoons chopped shallot
> 1 garlic clove, chopped
> 1¾ cups chicken broth
> ½ teaspoon salt
> 1 teaspoon curry powder
> ½ cup heavy cream or half-and-half

In a large heavy skillet over medium heat, cook zucchini until tender. Add shallot, garlic, chicken broth, salt, and curry powder for 15–20 minutes, stirring frequently.

Process in batches in blender until smooth.

If soup is to be served hot, reheat in a double boiler with cream. If soup is to be served icy cold, chill at least 6 hours or overnight. Stir in cream before serving.

Serves 4

Walker's Point Clam Chowder

½ cup salt pork, diced, rinds separated
½ cup chopped onion
1 pint shucked clams, chopped,
*   clam liquor reserved separately*
1 medium russet potato, peeled and diced
2 cups chicken broth
1 tablespoon unsalted butter
1 tablespoon all-purpose flour
2 cups light cream, heated
½ teaspoon salt
¼ teaspoon white pepper
2 tablespoons dry sherry

In a large heavy-bottomed saucepan over medium-high heat, cook pork rinds until dark brown and crisp. Remove pork rinds with slotted spoon onto paper towels and set aside. Cook remaining diced salt pork until crisp and dark brown. Remove with slotted spoon onto paper towels and set aside separately.

Pour off all but 1 tablespoon pork fat. In same saucepan, add onion and chopped clams and cook until onion is translucent. Add potato, chicken broth, clam liquor, and pork rinds and cook until potato is tender, about 5 minutes.

Transfer soup to double boiler over simmering water.

In a small saucepan over medium heat, melt butter. Add flour and cook, stirring, for 1 minute. Stirring constantly, add light cream and cook until thickened. Season with salt and white pepper. Add cream mixture to soup in double boiler and continue simmering.

Stir in sherry and serve immediately, garnished with reserved salt pork.

Serves 4

Walker's Point Fish Chowder

This chowder is especially good if it sits in the refrigerator overnight and is served the next day.

> 4 cups chicken broth
> 2 pounds skinless haddock fillet
> 2 cups thinly sliced peeled russet potatoes
> 1 (2-inch) cube salt pork, diced small
> 2 small onions, chopped
> 2 cups half-and-half
> Salt and pepper

In a stockpot over low heat, bring broth to a simmer. Add haddock and slowly poach until flaky. Remove fish with a slotted spoon and allow to cool slightly. Separate fish into chunky flakes. Discard bones, if any. Set aside.

In the same poaching liquid, add potatoes and boil until tender but firm. Remove stockpot from heat. Set aside.

In a heavy-bottomed saucepan over medium heat, fry salt pork until crisp. Remove with slotted spoon onto paper towels. Pour off all but 1 tablespoon pork fat. Divide salt pork. Set half of salt pork aside for garnish; return the other half to saucepan. Add onions and cook until translucent. Transfer potatoes, poaching liquid, and onions into top part of double boiler over simmering water.

Pour half-and-half into the saucepan and bring to a simmer. Pour into soup in double boiler. Continue simmering and gently stir in chunky fish flakes. Season with salt and pepper. Garnish with crisp salt pork.

Serves 8

Walker's Point Seafood Chowder

2 cups chicken broth
1 pound skinless haddock fillet
1 cup thinly sliced peeled potatoes (Yukon gold or red-skinned)
1 pound sea scallops, sliced
1 (2-inch) cube salt pork, diced small
2 (6-ounce) cans minced clams, with juice
1 small onion, chopped
¼ cup finely chopped celery
¼ cup diced red bell pepper
¼ cup finely diced carrot
4 cups half-and-half
White pepper
3 egg yolks, beaten
1 pound lobster meat, cut into chunks
Dry sherry, for serving

In a heavy saucepan over medium heat, bring broth to a simmer. Add haddock and slowly poach until flaky. Remove fish with a slotted spoon and allow to cool slightly. Separate fish into chunky flakes. Discard bones, if any. Set aside.

In the same poaching liquid, add potatoes and scallops and boil for about 5 minutes or until potatoes are tender but firm. Remove from heat and scoop out potatoes and scallops with slotted spoon and set aside. Transfer poaching liquid to top of double boiler over simmering water.

In a separate heavy-bottomed saucepan, fry salt pork until dark brown and crisp. Remove with slotted spoon onto paper towels. Pour off all but 1 tablespoon pork fat. Set half of salt pork aside for garnish; return the other half to saucepan. Add minced clams and clam juice, onion, celery, red bell pepper, and carrot and cook for about 3 minutes, or until vegetables are tender.

Add clam and vegetable mixture to poaching liquid in double boiler. Add potatoes and scallops mixture, half-and-half, and pepper and slowly simmer. A few minutes before serving time, add beaten egg yolks to hot soup and stir well until chowder begins to thicken. Add haddock to soup.

Ladle chowder into individual soup bowls and divide lobster among the bowls. Garnish with fried salt pork. Serve immediately. Offer dry sherry separately in a small pitcher to be drizzled over soup.

Serves 8

Senegalese Soup

Serve icy cold.

> 4 tablespoons unsalted butter
> 2 leeks, white parts only, sliced
> 2 celery stalks, sliced
> 1 onion, sliced
> 4 russet potatoes, peeled and thinly sliced
> 4 cups chicken broth
> 1 tablespoon salt
> 3 cups half-and-half
> 1 teaspoon curry powder
> 1 cup heavy cream
> 1 apple, peeled and finely chopped
> 1 cooked chicken breast, finely chopped

In a heavy-bottomed saucepan over medium heat, melt butter. Add leeks, celery, and onion and cook until onion is translucent. Add potatoes, chicken broth, and salt and simmer for 40 minutes. Work soup through food mill fitted with the fine disk. Discard solids.

Return soup to heat. Add half-and-half and curry powder and bring to a boil. Remove from heat, cool slightly, and strain again. When completely cool, add heavy cream. Chill thoroughly. Before serving, add apple and chicken.

Serves 8

SALADS

Jen's Broccoli Salad • Caesar Salad • Cobb Salad • Grandmother Pierce's
Creamy Salad Ring • Garden Salad with Walker's Point French Dressing •
Walker's Point French Dressing • Jicama Salad with Stilton Dressing •
Hearts of Palm and Avocado Salad • Chiffonade of Spinach •
Garlic Lemon Dressing • Chaparral Wilted Spinach Salad • Vegetable Salad •
Carolyn Deaver's Chinese Chicken Salad • Curried Chicken Salad •
Citrus Chicken Cashew Salad • Crab Louis

Carolyn Deaver's Chinese Chicken Salad

Jen's Broccoli Salad

This recipe was shared by Betty Hughes, the wife of Morris N. Hughes, Consul General in St. Petersburg. She named the salad after her daughter-in-law, Jennifer Lyn Kennedy. It became a popular salad entrée at the receptions held at the Consul General's residence. Confirmed non-broccoli eaters are reformed according to her.

I tested the salad, as instructed by Mrs. Barbara Bush, hoping it would also reform someone we knew. We served the salad elegantly during buffet service. Everyone—relatives and friends—was pleased and loved the broccoli salad. Our dear friend did pick up the bowl of broccoli salad, but only to pass the salad around for second helpings. Sorry, he is still not reformed.

1 large head broccoli, cut into bite-sized pieces
¼ cup chopped red onions
½ cup golden raisins
3 tablespoons white wine vinegar
2 tablespoons granulated sugar
       or sugar substitute
1 cup mayonnaise or Miracle Whip
5 slices bacon, fried, drained, and crumbled
1 cup sunflower seeds, toasted

In a large bowl, combine broccoli, red onions, and golden raisins. Set aside.

In another bowl, whisk together vinegar and sugar until dissolved. Add mayonnaise and blend well. Pour dressing over broccoli.

Toss until well mixed. Cover and refrigerate for at least 2 hours.

To serve, toss salad with half the crumbled bacon and half the sunflower seeds. Sprinkle remaining bacon and sunflower seeds on top as garnish.

Serves 4

Caesar Salad

FOR CROUTONS

4 tablespoons olive oil
3 garlic cloves, chopped
2 cups cubed (½-inch) bread, crusts removed
Grated Parmesan cheese

FOR DRESSING

3½ tablespoons lemon juice
1 tablespoon Worcestershire sauce
6 tablespoons olive oil
1 small egg
½ teaspoon salt
¼ teaspoon pepper
½ cup grated Parmesan cheese
¼ cup crumbled blue cheese

3 heads Romaine lettuce (hearts only), cut with a knife in even pieces

For croutons: In a small bowl, combine olive oil and garlic. Let sit at room temperature for at least 3 hours.

Heat oven to 350°.

Spread bread on baking sheet and bake for about 20 minutes, until golden brown. Wrap in wax paper and set aside.

For dressing: In a bowl, whisk together lemon juice, Worcestershire, olive oil, egg, salt, and pepper. Add cheeses and stir gently.

Strain and discard garlic from olive oil. Pour garlic-flavored olive oil over toasted bread and toss to coat well. Sprinkle with Parmesan cheese to taste and toss to coat croutons.

In a large salad bowl, toss lettuce with dressing. Add half the croutons and toss again. Garnish with remaining croutons.

Serves 4

Cobb Salad

Recent guests served this salad were Reba McEntire and her husband at the Bush residence in Houston. She had performed at the Houston rodeo and came over for lunch.

> 4 large eggs, hard-cooked
> 2 heads Bibb lettuce, cored and cut in half
> 2 medium tomatoes, cubed
> 4 ounces Cheddar cheese, cubed
> 16 pitted ripe olives, quartered
> 2 cooked whole chicken breasts, cubed
> 12 bacon slices, cut into large pieces,
>   cooked crisp
> Chopped parsley
> Assorted salad dressings, for serving

Cut eggs in half and separate yolks from whites. Mash yolks and slice whites.

Arrange lettuce on 4 individual plates. Arrange egg whites, tomatoes, Cheddar, olives, chicken, and bacon in spiraled layers. Sprinkle center of salad with mashed egg yolks. Sprinkle with chopped parsley.

Pass assorted salad dressings and allow diners to dress their own salads.

Serves 4

Grandmother Pierce's Creamy Salad Ring

This recipe has been passed down from Mrs. Barbara Bush's grandmother. The center can be filled with your favorite crab or shrimp salad or just with dressed lettuce.

3 cups canned diced tomatoes
3 tablespoons sugar
2 tablespoons onion juice
2 teaspoons salt
⅛ teaspoon pepper
2 tablespoons gelatin
⅓ cup cold water
½ cup diced cucumber
½ cup thinly sliced celery
½ cup chopped bell pepper
1 tablespoon prepared horseradish
½ cup heavy cream
1 cup mayonnaise

In a heavy-bottomed saucepan, bring tomatoes to a boil. Reduce heat and add sugar, onion juice, salt, and pepper and simmer for 10 minutes.

In a small bowl, soak gelatin in water until dissolved, blend, and mix well. Add this to hot tomato mixture to dissolve completely.

In a bowl, toss cucumber, celery, and bell pepper with horseradish. Add the tomato gelatin to the vegetables.

In a small bowl, beat heavy cream until stiff. Blend in mayonnaise. Immediately fold into tomato and vegetable mixture.

Pour into a well-buttered (or coated with pan spray) 12-inch ring mold. Chill thoroughly, at least 3 hours or overnight.

To serve, dip mold in hot water to loosen and invert on a serving tray. Carefully unmold ring. Fill center as desired.

Serves 12

Garden Salad
with Walker's Point French Dressing

2 bunches baby watercress
2 small heads red leaf lettuce
4 mozzarella balls, cut in half
1 red bell pepper, seeded
 and cut into strips
2 tablespoons pine nuts, toasted
2 tablespoons golden raisins
About ¾ cup Walker's Point French
 Dressing (page 73)
2 tablespoons chopped parsley

Discard wilted leaves, long stems, and roots of baby watercress. Separate leaves of leaf lettuce. Wash watercress and lettuce together under cold running water. Shake water off or spin-dry. Arrange greens on 4 salad plates, allowing a small space in the center of each arrangement. Fill each center with mozzarella halves, bell pepper strips, pine nuts, and golden raisins. Drizzle 3 tablespoons dressing over each plated salad and sprinkle with chopped parsley.

Serves 4

Garden Salad

Walker's Point French Dressing

1 (3.5-ounce) jar capers (do not drain)
3 Vidalia or other sweet onions, chopped
4 large garlic cloves, chopped
2 cups bottle-aged white wine vinegar
4 tablespoons honey
2 tablespoons Mrs. Dash salt substitute
2 tablespoons dried parsley, crushed
2 tablespoons dried basil, crushed
4 teaspoons salt
2 teaspoons black pepper
4 cups corn oil

In a food processor, pulse capers and their liquid until coarsely chopped. Add chopped onions and garlic and pulse until minced.

Evenly divide onions and capers mixture among 4 jars. Add ½ cup wine vinegar and 1 tablespoon honey to each jar. Add ½ tablespoon each of Mrs. Dash, parsley, and basil. Add 1 teaspoon salt and ½ teaspoon black pepper to each jar. Seal jars tightly and shake each jar to dissolve salt and mix ingredients well. Keep refrigerated overnight or longer to allow onion mixture to pickle and enhance its flavor. Only when ready to serve, add 1 cup corn oil per jar. Shake well.

The dressing will keep 1 month in the refrigerator.

Jicama Salad with Stilton Dressing

FOR DRESSING

2 ounces Stilton cheese
1 teaspoon honey
1 garlic clove
2 tablespoons white wine vinegar
2 tablespoons sour cream
¼ cup heavy cream
Salt and pepper

FOR SALAD

2 heads Belgian endive, petals separated from hard core,
*   sliced thinly lengthwise*
1 bunch watercress, stems trimmed
1 medium jicama, peeled and cut into matchsticks
1 small red onion, cut into thin rings
½ package alfalfa sprouts, rinsed and spin-dried

FOR GARNISH

1 ounce Stilton cheese, cubed
3 tablespoons pine nuts, toasted
12 grape or cherry tomatoes
2 tablespoons chopped cilantro

For dressing: In a blender, combine Stilton, honey, garlic, vinegar, and sour cream. With the machine running, slowly add heavy cream. Transfer to a bowl and season with salt and pepper. Cover and refrigerate until needed.

For salad: Arrange endive and watercress on 4 dinner plates. Lay jicama matchsticks and onion rings over salad. Arrange alfalfa sprouts like a bird's nest on the watercress. When ready to serve, drizzle each serving with 3 tablespoons dressing.

For garnish: Decorate salads with cheese, pine nuts, and tomatoes. Sprinkle with chopped cilantro.

Serves 4

Hearts of Palm and Avocado Salad

FOR DRESSING

1 teaspoon salt
1 teaspoon dried chervil
1 teaspoon chopped parsley
1 teaspoon Dijon-style mustard
1 teaspoon Worcestershire sauce
Juice of 1 lemon
3 garlic cloves, minced
½ teaspoon pepper
1½ cups extra virgin olive oil

FOR SALAD

1 large head iceberg lettuce, torn into bite-sized pieces
1 head red leaf lettuce, torn into bite-sized pieces
1 head Romaine lettuce, torn into bite-sized pieces
15 stuffed olives, halved
1 (14-ounce) can hearts of palm, drained
      and sliced into ¾-inch rounds
2 ripe avocados, seeded, peeled, and cubed
1¼ cups crumbled Feta cheese

For dressing: In a mixing bowl, whisk together salt, chervil, parsley, mustard, Worcestershire, lemon juice, garlic, and pepper. Whisk in olive oil to combine well. Set aside.

For salad: In a bowl, toss lettuce. Keep cold.

In another bowl, combine olives, hearts of palm, and avocados with ½ cup dressing.

When ready to serve, gradually pour dressing over lettuce and toss gently together with marinated ingredients. Gently stir in cheese.

Serves 8–10

During the summer of 1996, while in Kennebunkport, Maine, President (41) and Mrs. Bush took me out for a quiet dinner at the Salt Marsh Tavern. For a change, I didn't have to prepare their dinner that evening. I wined and dined, just the three of us. What a treat!

I was also on a mission that evening. Mrs. Bush wanted me to pay special attention to the salad she was going to order. She wanted my photographic memory to learn by heart all the ingredients that go into the salad. She wanted me to serve it at Walker's Point. I also ordered the spinach salad as a first course to find out how it tasted. Before Mrs. Bush took the first bite, and then between bites of salad, she would lean over to my side and whisper ingredients she identified. We kept dictating the ingredients to each other until we both finished our salads. Before the main course arrived, I excused myself and went to the restaurant kitchen. I met Executive Chef Rich Lemoine and complimented him on his superb spinach salad and let him know how everyone raved about it. As we were leaving the restaurant, the chef came out and shook the President's hand and bade good-bye to Mrs. Bush. He also handed me a copy of the recipe. I glanced at Mrs. Bush, who couldn't believe how easily I acquired the recipe. After all the secrecy, whispering, and spying, I just stood up, went to the kitchen, and asked for it. I did not have to tell her I used the President's name! Chef Rich was so generous, he willingly shared his prized menu item. It has become one of the most popular first courses at Walker's Point, at the Presidential Library at Texas A&M University, and at the Bush residence in Houston. Each time I serve the salad to high officials, dignitaries, heads of state, and our own current presidents, I know the salad has Salt Marsh Tavern written all over it.

Chiffonade of Spinach

2 red bell peppers, halved and seeded
2 bunches large leaf spinach, stemmed
and sliced thinly lengthwise
12 pitted Kalamata olives, quartered
4 ounces Feta cheese, diced
4 tablespoons pine nuts, toasted
Garlic Lemon Dressing (recipe follows)
4 tablespoons chopped parsley

Heat broiler. Place bell peppers cut side down on baking sheet. Broil peppers until skins turn black. Immediately place in brown paper bag and seal to trap steam to help remove roasted skins off peppers easily. Peel and cut into strips and set aside.

In a large bowl, toss spinach, roasted peppers, olives, cheese, and nuts with dressing.

Divide among 4 plates and sprinkle generously with chopped parsley, scattering on sides of plates as garnish.

Serves 4

Garlic Lemon Dressing

8 cloves garlic, roasted
Juice of 1 lemon
1 cup light olive oil
2 tablespoons honey
Salt and pepper
2 tablespoons chopped parsley

In a blender, combine garlic, lemon juice, oil, and honey. Pulse, turning blender on and off, to emulsify. Season with salt and pepper, add parsley, and pulse again.

Makes about 1¼ cups

Chaparral Wilted Spinach Salad

This salad is a favorite of President Bush (41).

> 3 cups spinach, washed, picked over,
> stems removed, spin-dried
> ½ cup diced bacon
> 3 tablespoons olive oil
> ½ cup diced onion
> ½ cup sliced mushrooms
> ¼ cup cognac
> 1 tablespoon Dijon-style mustard
> Juice of ½ lemon
> 2 tablespoons sour cream

Put spinach in a large bowl. Set aside.

In a skillet over medium heat, cook bacon until brown and crispy. Remove crispy bacon bits with slotted spoon; set aside. Discard bacon grease.

In the same skillet over medium heat, heat olive oil. Add onion and mushrooms and cook until mushrooms are tender. Remove from heat and pour in cognac. Return to heat and tip pan to ignite cognac. When flames die down, add mustard, lemon juice, and sour cream; stir well.

Pour hot dressing over spinach. Cover bowl with aluminum foil for 4 minutes until spinach wilts. Toss lightly and serve immediately.

Serves 4

Vegetable Salad

This recipe was shared by Patsy Caulkins, a friend of Mr. and Mrs. Bush from their days in New Haven.

FOR SALAD

1 pound fresh spinach, stems discarded
      and cut into shreds
5 eggs, hard-cooked and sliced
½ pound bacon, cooked and crumbled
½ head iceberg lettuce, shredded
½ cup sliced shallots
1 (10-ounce) package frozen baby peas,
      partially defrosted

FOR DRESSING

1¼ cups mayonnaise
1¼ cups sour cream
2 teaspoons Worcestershire sauce
Juice of ½ lemon
Salt and pepper
¾ cup grated Swiss cheese

For salad: In a large salad bowl, arrange in layers spinach, hard-cooked egg slices, bacon, iceberg lettuce, shallots, and peas.

For dressing: In a bowl, whisk together mayonnaise, sour cream, Worcestershire, and lemon juice. Season with salt and pepper.

Pour dressing over salad. Sprinkle top with cheese. Cover and chill for 12 hours.

Serve as is; do not toss.

Serves 8

Carolyn Deaver's Chinese Chicken Salad

This recipe was shared by Carolyn Deaver, a dear friend whose husband was in President Reagan's administration.

This is one of many favorite chicken salads served to visiting friends and guests. I keep notes to ensure that I don't serve this salad to the same guest twice during repeated visits. Former Prime Minister Margaret Thatcher visited then–Vice President George Bush, and I remembered this salad was offered. When he was President and Prime Minister Thatcher came for a bilateral meeting at Camp David, the culinary specialists assigned to Camp David proudly served the same chicken salad. I believe former Prime Minister Brian and Mrs. Mila Mulroney of Canada were also victims of duplication. General Colin Powell may think it is the only salad we know how to prepare.

FOR MARINADE

½ cup soy sauce
2 tablespoons sherry
3 tablespoons vegetable oil
3 tablespoons sugar
4 large chicken breast halves (bone in)

FOR DRESSING

4 tablespoons sugar
6 tablespoons balsamic vinegar
1 teaspoon salt
1 teaspoon black pepper
½ cup olive oil
2 tablespoons Asian sesame oil

Readers of Mrs. Barbara Bush's latest memoirs, *Reflections*, may find that she listed me on many pages, repeatedly mentioning how I prepared chicken salad. Readers may think that all I know how to prepare is one kind of chicken salad. You may find that this is not so.

6–8 cups vegetable oil
1 (8-ounce) package Oriental rice sticks

FOR SALAD

1 head iceberg lettuce, cut into ½-inch shreds
6 scallions, thinly sliced
4 tablespoons sesame seeds, toasted

For marinade: In a medium bowl, whisk soy sauce, sherry, oil, and sugar until well blended. Add chicken breasts and marinate in the refrigerator for at least 3 hours or overnight.

Heat oven to 350°.

Drain chicken breasts well, wrap individually in aluminum foil, place on baking sheets, and bake for 35 minutes. Allow chicken to cool, then remove and discard skin and bones and shred chicken meat into thin strips. Set aside.

For dressing: In a large bowl, dissolve sugar in balsamic vinegar. Stir in salt and pepper. In a steady stream, drizzle in olive oil while whisking vigorously to allow dressing to emulsify. Stir in sesame oil. Set aside. (I usually double the recipe to make sure I have enough to coat entire salad. Noodles tend to absorb dressing faster than the rest of the ingredients.)

For noodles: In a large heavy kettle, heat vegetable oil over medium-high heat. Test oil temperature by dipping in a rice stick. When stick puffs as soon as it touches oil, it's ready. Deep-fry rice sticks, a handful at a time, and quickly scoop out with slotted spoon from kettle as puffed sticks rise above oil. (Use slotted spoon to hold sticks under heated oil as they expand four times their size quickly. Flip upside down to fry sticks that missed the first frying process.) Lift sticks above oil with slotted spoon and allow oil to drain back into saucepan and then transfer puffed rice sticks to a large bowl double-lined with paper towels.

In a small bowl, toss together 1 cup shredded chicken, 1 tablespoon dressing, and 1 teaspoon sesame seeds. Set aside for garnish.

Just before serving the salad, in a very large bowl, combine lettuce, scallions, chicken, sesame seeds, and fried rice noodles. Toss together while lightly drizzling in dressing a little at a time. Divide salad among 4 plates and garnish with reserved chicken. Serve immediately. Noodles tend to absorb dressing and will wilt fast.

Serves 4

Curried Chicken Salad

FOR POACHING

4 cups chicken broth or water
1 celery stalk, cut in half
½ onion, cut into chunks
1 small carrot, diced
2 thin slices fresh ginger
½ teaspoon salt
⅛ teaspoon black whole peppercorns, cracked
2 whole chicken breasts (bone in) or 1 small turkey breast

FOR SALAD

1 cup golden raisins
2 (8-ounce) cans pineapple chunks, juice reserved
1 cup whole water chestnuts, quartered
1 cup green grapes, halved
½ cup chopped celery
¼ cup slivered almonds, lightly toasted
Shredded lettuce, for serving

FOR DRESSING

1 cup mayonnaise
3 tablespoons chutney
2 tablespoons honey

The Labuyo—inspiration for this carved pineapple—is a long-tailed, swift-flying wild rooster found in the mountains of the Philippines and other Asian countries.

Juice of ½ lemon
1 tablespoon sugar
½ teaspoon celery seed
1 teaspoon salt
1 tablespoon curry powder

For poaching: In a stockpot over medium heat, combine the broth, celery, onion, carrot, ginger, salt, peppercorns, and chicken breasts. Bring to a simmer and cook until chicken is tender, 35–40 minutes. Remove from heat and allow chicken to cool. Pull meat from bones and shred into thin strips. Set aside. Discard skin and bones. Reserve stock for another use.

For salad: While chicken cooks, in a bowl, combine raisins and reserved pineapple juice to allow raisins to plump slightly. In a large bowl, combine water chestnuts, grapes, celery, almonds, and pineapple chunks. Keep chilled.

For dressing: In a bowl, whisk together mayonnaise, chutney, honey, lemon juice, sugar, celery seed, salt, and curry powder. Set aside.

In 1997, Sharon Bush visited Mrs. Barbara Bush in Houston and brought this salad. The former First Lady helped herself to the salad at lunchtime and was so delighted by the flavor and richness of the dish that she decided to have it again for dinner. The whole time we were in Houston, Mrs. Bush raved about Sharon's chicken salad.

While at Walker's Point the following summer, Sharon arrived with Lauren, Pierce, and Ashley—and a piece of paper with a list of ingredients. She claimed Mrs. Bush begged her to share her renowned Curried Chicken Salad recipe with me so I could start serving the dish to guests at Walker's Point.

As she was pulling away to head out to New Hampshire to visit her relatives, I glanced at the note. It read, "Chicken, Water chestnuts, Grapes, Pineapple chunks, Almonds, Raisins, Lemon, Mayonnaise, and Curry powder." No other entries, no measurements, no procedures to follow.

So I tested, experimented, and added my own variations. This is what I came up with, and I have served Curried Chicken Salad to numerous guests at Walker's Point, in Houston, and at the George Bush Presidential Library at Texas A&M.

Drain raisins, discarding juice, and add raisins and chicken to salad ingredients. Toss with dressing. Cover and refrigerate for at least 2 hours before serving.

Serve on beds of shredded lettuce.

Serves 8

Citrus Chicken Cashew Salad

FOR DRESSING

½ cup cilantro
¼ cup parsley
¼ cup olive oil
¼ cup orange juice
1½ teaspoons red wine vinegar
1½ tablespoons Dijon-style mustard
1 teaspoon salt
2 teaspoons sugar
⅛ teaspoon pepper

FOR SALAD

1⅓ cups cooked and shredded
chicken breast
3 celery stalks, sliced
½ head Romaine lettuce,
torn into bite-sized pieces
4 scallions, sliced diagonally
1 large red bell pepper, seeded
and cut into thin strips

¼ cup roasted cashew nuts

For dressing: In a blender combine cilantro, parsley, oil, juice, vinegar, mustard, salt, sugar, and pepper. Puree until smooth. Refrigerate until ready to use.

For salad: In a large bowl, combine chicken, celery, lettuce, scallions, and bell pepper.

When ready to serve, toss salad and dressing together and sprinkle top with cashews.

Serves 4

Crab Louis

FOR DRESSING

1 egg yolk
2 teaspoons Dijon-style mustard
½ teaspoon Worcestershire sauce
2 teaspoons red wine vinegar
Salt and pepper
½ cup extra virgin olive oil
1 tablespoon chili sauce

FOR SALAD

¼ cup chopped scallions
4 large stuffed green olives, chopped
1 pound lump crabmeat, picked over
Assorted lettuce leaves, for serving
Sliced hard-cooked eggs, for serving (optional)

For dressing: In a mixing bowl, beat yolk, mustard, Worcestershire, vinegar, and salt and pepper. Add olive oil gradually, beating rapidly with a whisk. When thickened and smooth, add chili sauce and blend well.

For salad: In a bowl, combine scallions, olives, and crabmeat. Add half the dressing and blend gently so as not to break up crab lumps more than necessary.

Arrange assorted lettuce leaves nicely on 4 large salad plates. Divide crab among plates. Spoon remaining dressing over leaves. Garnish with egg slices, if desired.

Serves 4

CHICKEN

Baked Chicken Breasts • Chicken Cordon Bleu • Baked Breaded Chicken •
Stuffed Chicken Breasts • Portuguese Sauce • Chicken Combo •
Chicken Kiev • Madeira Sauce • Stuffed Chicken Legs • Sauce Chasseur •
Chicken à la King • Biscuit Ring • Creamed Chicken • Paula's Lemon Chicken •
Chengtu Chicken • Garlic Chicken • Chicken Satay with Peanut Sauce •
Cashew Chicken • Spicy Chicken with Scallions • Chicken Adobo •
Almond Chicken • Chicken Curry

Chicken Adobo (Brush-on Method)

Baked Chicken Breasts

Mrs. Barbara Bush has kept this recipe, shared by Patsy Caulkins, in the family's cookbook for years. It is the simplest way to bake chicken. It brings back memories of the days she and Mr. Bush lived with Mrs. Caulkins and her husband in New Haven, Connecticut, at Yale University in 1945, along with eleven other families in a big house divided into small apartments.

1 (1.25-ounce) package onion soup mix
1 (10.5-ounce) can mushroom soup
1 pint sour cream
1 tablespoon dry vermouth
4 boneless, skinless chicken breast halves

Heat oven to 325°.

In a large bowl, blend soup mix, mushroom soup, sour cream, and vermouth together. Add chicken breasts and toss to coat all pieces. Arrange chicken in a casserole dish. Scrape in any soup mixture left in bowl and level top with rubber spatula.

Bake, uncovered, for 2 hours.

Serves 4

VARIATION

Dark meat may be used, with or without skin and bones.

Chicken Cordon Bleu

FOR DIPPING

2 egg whites
½ teaspoon grated nutmeg
½ teaspoon paprika
Salt and pepper

FOR CRUMBS

2 cups plain bread crumbs
4 tablespoons grated Parmesan cheese
4 (6-ounce) boneless, skinless, chicken breasts
(see Note)

FOR STUFFING

4 thick slices Swiss cheese
4 thick slices ham

4 tablespoons unsalted butter,
plus additional as needed

Heat oven to 375°.

For dipping: In a large bowl, whisk together egg whites, nutmeg, paprika, and salt and pepper until frothy. Set aside.

For crumbs: In a flat bowl, combine bread crumbs and Parmesan cheese. Set aside.

Using meat pounder, gently flatten each chicken breast between two sheets of plastic wrap, being careful not to tear breast meat. Remove plastic and, with a knife, slice into the side of each chicken breast to make an inside pocket.

Stuff each chicken breast with 1 slice Swiss cheese and 1 slice ham. Close opening completely, making sure ham and cheese are not exposed.

Dip the chicken into the egg mixture; drain excess. Coat all sides of chicken entirely and evenly with the crumb mixture.

In a large skillet over low heat, slowly heat butter. Add chicken breasts and fry on low heat until browned, about 3 minutes on each side. Add more butter for frying, as needed.

Transfer to baking dish and bake for 15 minutes.

Serves 4

Note: For an extra touch, I butcher chickens myself. First split the chicken evenly in half lengthwise. Cut away back and leg from each half (save for another use). Cut off wing tips, but do not cut chicken wings from breast. Bone the breast halves and remove skins. Leave bones in drumette; these will serve as handles.

Baked Breaded Chicken

½ cup grated Parmesan cheese
2 cups plain bread crumbs
3 tablespoons sesame seeds
½ cup margarine or unsalted butter,
*   plus additional*
6–8 pounds boneless, skinless chicken
*   breast halves*
Sweet and Spicy Sauce (page 208),
*   for serving*

In a plastic bag, mix Parmesan cheese, bread crumbs, and sesame seeds together. Set aside.

In a saucepan over low heat, melt margarine. Add chicken and toss to coat all over. Transfer coated chicken to plastic bag with bread crumb mixture and shake well.

Freeze breaded chicken for 30–60 minutes.

When ready to bake, bring breaded chicken to room temperature.

Heat oven to 350º.

Place chicken on baking sheet and dot with margarine. Bake for 1 hour. Serve with Sweet and Spicy Sauce.

Serves 6–8

Stuffed Chicken Breasts

This recipe was introduced to the Vice President's kitchen staff by Laurie Firestone, Social Secretary to Mrs. Barbara Bush, during Mr. Bush's tenure as Vice President and as 41st President. The origin of the recipe is unknown.

The finished dish is very eye appealing when I prepare it. Cut the chicken into halves and serve with a hearty salad. It has become one of many family favorite dishes.

You can ask your butcher to bone the chicken breasts, leaving the skin on, or you can do it yourself.

1 tablespoon unsalted butter
8 scallions, finely chopped
¼ cup chopped parsley
1 teaspoon dried chervil
1 tablespoon chopped fresh oregano
1 tablespoon chopped dill
Salt and pepper
1 (10-ounce) package frozen spinach,
      defrosted and drained well
½ cup shelled unsalted pistachios
¼ cup diced roasted red bell pepper
1 large egg, lightly beaten
1 (15-ounce) container low-fat ricotta cheese
8 chicken breast halves, bone in and skin on
Paprika
Garlic salt
Portuguese Sauce (recipe follows), for serving

Heat oven to 350º. Grease a 13 x 9-inch baking dish.

In a saucepan over medium heat, melt butter. Add scallions and cook until tender. Blend in parsley, chervil, oregano, dill, salt and pepper to taste, and spinach. Cook for 3 minutes. Remove from heat and allow mixture to cool; stir in pistachios and diced roasted bell pepper. Set aside.

In a small bowl, mix egg and ricotta cheese until well blended. Blend ricotta cheese mixture with spinach mixture. Divide the stuffing into 8 equal portions and chill while preparing the chicken breast halves.

Rinse chicken breast halves and pat dry with paper towels. Bone breasts, leaving skin on.

Gently loosen skin from one side of the breast. Stuff a portion of stuffing under skin of each breast. Stretch skin over stuffing and tuck under the breast, forming even dome shapes. Arrange chicken, skin side up, in baking dish. Sprinkle with paprika and garlic salt.

Bake for 45–55 minutes, until well cooked. Check by cutting a breast from the center of the baking dish in half. If underdone, rearrange chicken in dishes, switching inside pieces with outside, and return to oven. Remove chicken from pan and tent with foil to keep warm. Save drippings for Portuguese Sauce.

To serve, slice breasts in half, exposing stuffing. Drizzle sauce around the chicken.

Serves 8

Portuguese Sauce

> 1 teaspoon olive oil
> 1 garlic clove, minced
> 1 scallion, finely chopped
> 1 tablespoon all-purpose flour
> $\frac{2}{3}$ cup drippings (from Stuffed Chicken Breasts)
> 4 ripe tomatoes, peeled, seeded, and chopped
> $\frac{1}{4}$ teaspoon salt
> $\frac{1}{8}$ teaspoon pepper
> 1 tablespoon tomato paste
> 2 teaspoons chopped parsley

In a saucepan over medium heat, heat oil. Add garlic and scallion and cook until tender. Stir in flour and cook, stirring constantly, until flour browns, about 3 minutes. Stir in drippings and cook, stirring, until the sauce thickens. Add tomatoes and cook until softened. Season with salt and pepper, stir in tomato paste and parsley, and bring to a simmer. Cook 2 minutes.

Makes about 2 cups

Chicken Combo

This chicken and stuffing combination is very popular with Mrs. Barbara Bush's friends; it may be prepared a day ahead.

FOR POACHING

8 chicken breast halves, bone in and skin on
5 cups water
1 carrot, sliced
2 celery stalks, sliced
1 small onion, quartered
2 slices fresh ginger
½ teaspoon pepper
4 chicken bouillon cubes

FOR SAUCE

4 tablespoons unsalted butter
1 cup chopped onion
½ cup chopped celery
½ cup chopped carrots
4 tablespoons all-purpose flour
2 cups finely chopped mushrooms
1 cup light cream
16 ounces sour cream
1 tablespoon curry powder

FOR TOPPING

1 teaspoon poultry seasoning
½ teaspoon dried thyme
1 (1-pound) package ready-mix poultry stuffing

For poaching: In a stockpot over high heat, combine chicken breast halves, water, carrot, celery, onion, ginger, pepper, and bouillon cubes. Bring to a rolling boil for 3 minutes. Reduce heat to medium-low and simmer for 25 minutes. Strain, reserving broth and vegetables; discard ginger slices. Set chicken aside. Skim fat from broth. Reserve broth.

Discard ginger slices and work vegetables through food mill. Combine puree with 2 cups broth and set aside for sauce.

When chicken is cool enough to handle, discard skin and bones. Cut chicken into bite-sized pieces and place in a 13 x 9-inch baking dish. Set aside.

Heat oven to 350°.

For sauce: In a saucepan over medium heat, melt butter. Add onion, celery, and carrots and cook until tender. Add flour and cook, stirring, until flour browns, about 3 minutes. Add mushrooms and cook, stirring often, until tender. Stir in 2 cups reserved broth mixture and light cream and cook, stirring often, until sauce is very thick. Fold in sour cream and curry powder. The sauce should have the consistency of pancake batter. Spread over chicken and set aside.

For topping: In a large bowl, blend poultry seasoning, thyme, and stuffing mix. Pour in about 2 cups broth, ½ cup at a time, stirring until dry ingredients have absorbed broth and are completely moistened. Add more broth if too dry. Spread topping over chicken and sauce, covering completely, and bake for 35–40 minutes, until bubbling.

Serves 12

Note: Dark meat lovers may substitute chicken legs and thighs for chicken breasts.

Chicken Kiev

If I were asked if I had any signature dishes, I would have to say Chicken Kiev and Chicken Cordon Bleu (page 89).

> 8 tablespoons (1 stick) unsalted butter, softened
> 1 garlic clove, minced
> Juice of 1 lemon
> ¼ cup chopped parsley
> 2 tablespoons chopped chives
> 1 teaspoon pepper
> 1 tablespoon brandy
> 2 boneless chicken breast halves, skin on,
>   drumette attached (see Note, page 90)
> 1 egg
> ½ cup milk
> 1 cup seasoned bread crumbs
> 4 cups vegetable oil
> Madeira Sauce (recipe follows), for serving

In a food processor or stand mixer, combine butter, garlic, lemon juice, parsley, chives, pepper, and brandy. Process or beat to combine. Scrape butter onto a piece of plastic wrap and form into a flat block. Wrap in plastic and freeze for at least 5 minutes, until very firm.

Place chicken between two sheets of plastic wrap and gently pound boneless meat only to flatten it.

Divide butter into 2 pieces and wrap chicken around butter. The chicken must encase the butter completely, and the drumette should be sticking up. Place on a plate and freeze for 15 minutes.

In a bowl, beat egg and milk together until well mixed. Pour bread crumbs onto a plate.

Dip chicken into egg, let excess drip off, and coat with bread crumbs. Return to freezer for 15 minutes. Repeat breading; dip in egg and coat in crumbs. Return to freezer for at least 15 minutes.

Heat oven to 350º. In a saucepan, heat oil to 375º.

Deep-fry chicken until lightly and evenly browned. Transfer to a small baking dish and bake for 15 minutes. Remove chicken from baking dish and keep warm. Save drippings for Madeira Sauce.

Serve breasts whole, or sliced on the diagonal, with the sauce.

Serves 2

Madeira Sauce

> 4 tablespoons unsalted butter
>   or drippings from Chicken Kiev
> ½ onion, sliced
> 2 tablespoons all-purpose flour
> 1 cup chicken broth
> 6 tablespoons Madeira
> Salt and pepper

In a saucepan over low heat, melt 2 tablespoons butter. Add onion and cook until lightly browned. Remove onion with slotted spoon, leaving butter in pan. Discard onion. Add flour and cook, stirring constantly, until flour is browned. Remove from heat and stir in broth and 5 tablespoons Madeira. Return to heat and cook, stirring often, until reduced to about 1 cup. Stir in remaining 2 tablespoons butter. Keep warm.

When ready to serve, stir in remaining 1 tablespoon Madeira.

Makes about 1 cup

Stuffed Chicken Legs

8 large whole chicken legs (thigh and drumstick)
Salt and pepper
½ pound chicken livers
4 tablespoons unsalted butter
3 tablespoons chopped shallot
3 cups finely chopped mushrooms
Juice of 1 lemon
¾ cup dry white wine
1 teaspoon chopped sage
1 teaspoon chopped thyme
½ teaspoon dry marjoram
2 large eggs, beaten
1 cup seasoned bread crumbs
Sauce Chasseur (recipe follows), for serving

Bone out thighs and drumsticks, being careful not to tear meat or skin. With a cleaver, cut drumstick bone, leaving the tip intact. Season with salt and pepper and refrigerate until needed.

Heat the broiler and spray a baking sheet with pan spray.

Rinse chicken livers in cool water and pat dry with paper towels. Place on baking sheet and broil for 3 minutes, until blistered and browned. Turn livers over and broil until other side is browned. Transfer livers to food processor and pulse to chop coarsely (or chop by hand). Set aside.

In a saucepan over medium heat, melt 3 tablespoons butter. Add shallot, mushrooms, lemon juice, and wine and cook, stirring often, until liquid has reduced and pan is almost dry. Stir in sage, thyme, marjoram, and chicken livers. Season with salt and pepper and cook for 5 minutes. Remove from heat and stir in eggs and bread crumbs. Transfer to a bowl and refrigerate until chilled.

Heat oven to 350°. Spray a baking sheet with pan spray.

Stuff boned chicken with stuffing, securing the skin with a toothpick if necessary. Arrange chicken, skin side up, on baking sheet and reshape to resemble bone-in whole legs. Dot with remaining 1 tablespoon butter. Bake for 40 minutes.

Serve with Sauce Chasseur.

Serves 8

Sauce Chasseur

> *2 tablespoons unsalted butter*
> *1 tablespoon vegetable oil*
> *1 cup sliced mushrooms (stems discarded)*
> *Salt and pepper*
> *1 tablespoon chopped scallion*
> *1 tablespoon brandy*
> *4 cups white wine*
> *1 tablespoon all-purpose flour*
> *½ cup beef broth*
> *1 tablespoon tomato paste*
> *1 tablespoon chopped parsley*

In a medium saucepan over medium heat, melt butter in oil. Add mushrooms and cook until light brown. Add salt and pepper, scallion, brandy, and white wine. Simmer until liquid is reduced by half. Dissolve flour completely in beef broth. Add to saucepan, stirring until thickened. Stir in tomato paste and parsley.

Makes about 2½ cups

Stuffed Chicken Leg

Chicken à la King

You could also serve this over fluffy steamed rice.

> 8 tablespoons (1 stick) unsalted butter
> 1/4 cup chopped onion
> 1/2 cup sliced mushrooms
> 1/4 cup thinly sliced green bell pepper
> 1/4 cup chopped celery
> 6 tablespoons all-purpose flour
> 1 teaspoon salt
> 1/8 teaspoon white pepper
> 2 tablespoons dry sherry
> 1 1/2 cups chicken broth
> 1 cup heavy cream
> 2 cups diced cooked chicken
> 1/4 cup sliced pimiento
> Biscuit Ring (recipe follows), for serving

In a saucepan over medium heat, melt butter. Add onion, mushrooms, bell pepper, and celery and cook until tender. Blend in flour, salt, and pepper. Cook over low heat until smooth and bubbly.

Remove from heat and stir in sherry, broth, and cream. Return to heat and bring to a boil for 1 minute, stirring constantly. Gently stir in chicken and pimiento and cook for 1 minute to heat chicken.

To serve, set Biscuit Ring on platter. Spoon chicken into center.

Serves 8

VARIATION

Follow above recipe, substituting 1 cup diced cooked ham for 1 cup chicken.

Biscuit Ring

This flavored biscuit ring complements Creamed Chicken and Chicken à la King perfectly.

> 2¼ cups all-purpose flour
> 5 teaspoons baking powder
> ½ teaspoon salt
> 1 teaspoon poultry seasoning
> ⅓ cup vegetable shortening
> 1 cup milk

Heat oven to 450°. Lightly grease a 12-inch ring mold.

In a bowl, sift flour, baking powder, salt, and poultry seasoning together. Cut in shortening until mixture resembles fine crumbs. Mix in milk thoroughly. Fill ring mold with dough. Bake for 15 minutes.

Unmold on hot serving platter. Serve hot with hot Creamed Chicken or Chicken à la King in center.

Makes one 12-inch biscuit ring

Creamed Chicken

You can also serve this dish with toast points or fluffy white rice.

6 tablespoons unsalted butter
6 tablespoons all-purpose flour
1 teaspoon salt
$\frac{1}{8}$ teaspoon white pepper
1½ cups chicken broth
1 cup heavy cream
2 cups diced cooked chicken
2 tablespoons dry sherry
Biscuit Ring (page 101), for serving

In a heavy-bottomed saucepan over low heat, melt butter. Blend in flour, salt, and pepper. Cook over low heat until smooth and bubbly. Remove from heat and stir in broth and cream. Return to heat and bring to a boil for 1 minute, stirring constantly.

Stir in chicken and cook for 1 minute to heat through. Remove from heat. Stir in sherry.

To serve, set Biscuit Ring on platter. Spoon chicken into center.

Serves 4

Paula's Lemon Chicken

We call this recipe the "daughters-in-law's favorite." Margaret Bush, Columba Bush, and Laura Bush have all asked for the recipe after being introduced to it at Walker's Point. The First Lady Laura added this to her recipe collection at the Governor's Mansion in Austin during George W. Bush's tenure as governor of Texas. Margaret often prepares this dish to entertain Marvin and her guests at their house in Alexandria, Virginia. Columba specifically asked for this recipe so the dish could be prepared by the chef at the Governor's Mansion in Tallahassee, Florida.

6 boneless, skinless chicken breast halves,
    sliced into 4 pieces each
Salt and pepper
½ cup all-purpose flour
8 tablespoons (1 stick) unsalted butter
2 tablespoons dry vermouth
2 tablespoons lemon juice
3 cups heavy cream
¼ teaspoon grated lemon zest
Grated Parmesan cheese

Heat oven to 350°. Season chicken with salt and pepper and dust lightly with flour.

In a large skillet over medium heat, melt butter. Fry chicken until golden brown on each side. Transfer chicken to a 13 x 9-inch baking dish.

Discard all but 1 tablespoon butter from skillet. Return to heat and add vermouth and lemon juice. Bring to boil. Stir in cream, lemon zest, and salt and pepper to taste. Simmer until sauce begins to thicken. Pour evenly over chicken. Sprinkle with Parmesan cheese to taste and bake for 30 minutes, until bubbly.

Serves 6

Chengtu Chicken

FOR MARINADE

1 teaspoon dry sherry
1 tablespoon soy sauce
1 egg white, lightly beaten
2/3 pound boneless, skinless chicken breast,
      cut into 1-inch cubes

FOR SEASONING SAUCE

1 teaspoon dry sherry
1 tablespoon soy sauce
1½ teaspoons sugar
1 teaspoon rice vinegar
2 tablespoons chicken broth
2 teaspoons oyster sauce
1 teaspoon cornstarch
2 tablespoons water
Salt and pepper

TO FINISH

1 cup vegetable oil
2/3 pound spinach
Salt
1 teaspoon chopped fresh ginger
1 tablespoon chopped garlic
1 tablespoon chopped scallion
1 tablespoon hot bean sauce
1 teaspoon sesame oil

For marinade: In a bowl, mix sherry, soy sauce, and egg white. Add chicken, mix well, and marinate for at least 20 minutes.

For seasoning sauce: In a bowl, mix sherry, soy sauce, sugar, vinegar, broth, oyster sauce, cornstarch, water, and salt and pepper to taste. Set aside.

To finish: In a wok over high heat, heat oil until smoking. Stir-fry chicken for 1 minute, until very lightly browned. Scoop out chicken with slotted spoon and set aside. Pour off oil, reserving 4 tablespoons.

Spoon 2 tablespoons oil into wok, still over high heat. Add spinach and salt and stir-fry until spinach is wilted and tender. Remove spinach with slotted spoon and arrange in a ring on serving platter.

Wipe out wok and return to high heat. Add 2 tablespoons oil and heat to smoking. Add ginger, garlic, scallion, and bean sauce and stir-fry for 1–2 minutes. Return chicken to wok and add seasoning sauce. Stir-fry until sauce thickens, about 1 minute. Stir in sesame oil and cook for 1 minute.

Spoon chicken into center of spinach ring.

Serves 4

When President and Mrs. Bush request an Asian meal (see page 116), Chengtu Chicken, Garlic Chicken, Chicken Satay with Peanut Sauce, Cashew Chicken, or Spicy Chicken with Scallions will be one of the many dishes to savor.

Garlic Chicken

1 teaspoon dry sherry
¼ teaspoon salt
1 tablespoon sesame oil
1 egg white, lightly beaten
1 pound boneless, skinless chicken breast,
     cut into 2-inch pieces
1 cup vegetable oil

FOR VEGETABLES AND SAUCE

¼ cup chopped garlic
¼ cup thinly sliced carrots
¼ cup sliced bamboo shoots
⅓ cup sliced water chestnuts
½ teaspoon salt
½ teaspoon sugar
3 tablespoons soy sauce
½ cup water

TO FINISH

¼ cup cornstarch, dissolved in 3 tablespoons
     chicken stock
1 teaspoon sesame oil

For marinade: In a bowl, mix sherry, salt, sesame oil, and egg white. Add chicken and stir to coat well. Allow chicken to marinate for at least 20 minutes.

Heat oil in wok over high heat. Stir-fry chicken for 3–4 minutes until almost cooked. Remove with slotted spoon, draining well over wok; set aside. Pour off all but 4 tablespoons oil.

For vegetables and sauce: Add garlic and carrots to wok and stir-fry for 30 seconds. Add bamboo shoots and water chestnuts and stir-fry for 1 minute. Add chicken, salt, sugar, soy sauce, and water, cover, and cook for 10 minutes.

To finish: Add the cornstarch paste to the chicken and vegetable mixture. Stir-fry until sauce thickens slightly, about 30 seconds. Stir in sesame oil.

Serves 4

Chicken Satay with Peanut Sauce

Serve with steamed rice and grilled vegetables, such as white onions, zucchini, mushrooms, and cherry tomatoes.

You may also serve Chicken Satay on skewers, without the vegetables and rice, as an appetizer, using Peanut Sauce as a dip.

FOR MARINADE

½ cup soy sauce
¼ cup brown sugar, packed
2 tablespoons lemon juice
¼ cup vegetable oil
1 teaspoon ground ginger
½ teaspoon garlic powder
1 pound boneless, skinless chicken breast,
      cut into thin 1½ x 2-inch strips

FOR PEANUT SAUCE

2 tablespoons peanut oil
½ cup sliced yellow onion
1 cup creamy peanut butter
½ cup light soy sauce
Dash of Tabasco
Dash of garlic powder
2 tablespoons brown sugar
1 tablespoon lemon juice

For marinade: In a bowl, combine soy sauce, sugar, lemon juice, oil, ginger, and garlic. Add chicken, cover, and marinate several hours or overnight in the refrigerator.

For peanut sauce: In a saucepan over medium heat, heat oil. Add onion and cook until translucent. Add peanut butter, soy sauce, Tabasco, garlic powder, brown sugar, and lemon juice and cook, stirring, until smooth. Keep sauce warm.

Prepare an outdoor grill or heat broiler.

Thread chicken strips onto skewers. Grill on barbecue pit or broil in the oven. Serve with Peanut Sauce.

Serves 4

Cashew Chicken

The cashews, made on their own, are a delicious snack. Store them in a tightly covered container.

FOR MARINADE

¼ teaspoon salt
⅛ teaspoon pepper
1 teaspoon cornstarch
1 tablespoon soy sauce
1 large egg
2 pounds boneless, skinless chicken thighs,
      cut into 1-inch cubes

FOR SEASONING SAUCE

1 tablespoon dry sherry
2 tablespoons soy sauce
1 tablespoon rice vinegar
1 tablespoon sugar
½ teaspoon salt
½ teaspoon cornstarch

4 cups vegetable oil
1 cup blanched cashews

TO FINISH

5 slices fresh ginger
3 scallions, cut into 1-inch pieces
1 green bell pepper, seeded and cut into 1-inch pieces
½ cup sliced bamboo shoots

For marinade: In a bowl combine salt, pepper, cornstarch, soy sauce, and egg and stir to dissolve the cornstarch. Add chicken and marinate for at least 30 minutes.

For seasoning sauce: In a small bowl, combine sherry, soy sauce, vinegar, sugar, salt, and cornstarch. Set aside.

For cashews: In a wok over medium heat, heat oil to 350°. Add cashews and fry, stirring constantly, for 10 minutes. Remove with a slotted spoon. Drain well on paper towels. Pour off oil, reserving 1 cup.

To finish: In a wok over high heat, heat reserved 1 cup oil to smoking. Stir-fry chicken for 2 minutes. Remove chicken with slotted spoon, draining well over wok; set aside.

Pour off all but 2 tablespoons oil. Reheat oil in wok over medium heat and stir-fry ginger for 30 seconds; remove ginger slices and discard. Add scallions, bell pepper, and bamboo shoots and stir-fry for 2 minutes.

Add seasoning sauce and bring to a boil. Add chicken to boiling sauce and mix to coat well. Add crisp cashews. Mix well. Serve hot.

Serves 8

Spicy Chicken with Scallions

FOR SEASONING SAUCE

1 tablespoon dry sherry
2 tablespoons soy sauce
1 tablespoon sugar
1 teaspoon salt
1 teaspoon cornstarch
1 teaspoon sesame oil

FOR CHICKEN

2 tablespoons cornstarch
1 tablespoon soy sauce
2 pounds boneless, skinless chicken thighs,
    cut into 1-inch pieces
1 cup vegetable oil
10 dried hot red peppers, stems removed
1 teaspoon peppercorns
1 teaspoon minced fresh ginger
½ cup chopped roasted peanuts
1 bunch scallions, cut into 1-inch pieces
1 teaspoon hot pepper flakes

For seasoning sauce: In a bowl, mix sherry, soy sauce, sugar, salt, cornstarch, and sesame oil. Set aside.

For chicken: In a bowl, mix cornstarch and soy sauce. Add chicken and toss to coat.

In a wok over high heat, heat oil to smoking. Add chicken and stir-fry for 2 minutes. Remove chicken with slotted spoon, draining well over wok. Set aside.

Pour off all but 2 tablespoons oil. Reheat oil to smoking and add hot peppers and peppercorns. Stir-fry until peppers turn dark brown. Add ginger and cook for 30 seconds. Return chicken to wok with seasoning sauce and cook, stirring, until sauce thickens slightly. Remove from heat and stir in peanuts, scallions, and hot pepper flakes.

Serves 8

Chicken Adobo

1 (2½ to 3-pound) chicken
½ cup rice vinegar
¼ cup soy sauce
10–15 whole black peppercorns, cracked
6 garlic cloves, crushed
2 bay leaves
2 teaspoons cornstarch
2 teaspoons sugar
1 tablespoon water
2 tablespoons unsalted butter

Cut chicken into 8 serving pieces; rinse in cold water.

In a heavy-bottomed saucepan, combine chicken, vinegar, soy sauce, peppercorns, and garlic. Toss to coat all chicken pieces. Add bay leaves. Cover and simmer for 25 minutes. Remove saucepan from heat. Transfer chicken pieces from saucepan to a medium bowl with a slotted spoon, draining sauce back to saucepan. Set chicken aside. Discard bay leaves.

In a measuring cup, combine cornstarch, sugar, and water; stir to make smooth paste. Stir into hot sauce in saucepan. Return to heat and cook until sauce begins to thicken; cook until reduced by half. Add butter gradually and stir until melted. Return chicken pieces to sauce and simmer for 5 minutes (stir only once during the entire cooking process to keep chicken meat intact and not pulled from bones). Transfer chicken pieces to serving platter, arranging each in its proper place to resemble a butterflied chicken. Drizzle sauce over chicken pieces.

Serves 4

VARIATION

Dark Meat Chicken Adobo: Follow above recipe using chicken thighs, drumsticks, or wings—or a combination.

Brush-on Method

Heat oven to 375º.

Follow Adobo recipe, except boil chicken pieces for 5 minutes only in vinegar, soy sauce, black peppercorns, garlic, and bay leaves. Remove chicken from pot and arrange on sheet pan; set aside.

Boil sauce until reduced by half and bubbly. Make paste with cornstarch, sugar, and water and add to hot sauce. Continue stirring until sauce has thickened. Add 3 tablespoons unsalted butter. Stir to blend well. Remove pan from heat and brush chicken generously with sauce. Bake for 20 minutes and continue brushing and basting with remaining sauce. Reduce heat to 300º and bake for 10 minutes more, or until chicken is tender.

Serves 4

Almond Chicken

At times, I serve this over fluffy rice, but I will also accompany it with biscuits or large toasted English muffins.

> 2 tablespoons vegetable oil
> 2 boneless, skinless chicken breasts,
>   cut into chunks
> ½ cup sliced mushrooms
> ½ cup sliced bamboo shoots
> ½ cup sliced water chestnuts
> 2 cups sliced (on the diagonal) celery
> ½ cup sugar snap peas
> Salt
> 2 tablespoons cornstarch
> 2 cups chicken broth
> ½ cup almonds, toasted

In a heavy-bottomed saucepan over medium-high heat, heat oil. Add chicken and cook, stirring until very lightly browned. Add mushrooms, bamboo shoots, water chestnuts, celery, and sugar snap peas, season with salt, and sauté for 5 minutes. Set aside. Keep warm.

Dissolve cornstarch in some of the broth. Place in saucepan with remaining broth and bring to a simmer, stirring constantly until sauce thickens. Boil for 1 minute. Add chicken and vegetables and simmer for 5 minutes more. Serve with toasted almonds.

Serves 2

Chicken Curry

This is equally delicious made with turkey.

> 8 tablespoons (1 stick) unsalted butter
> 2 cups chopped mushrooms
> 1 onion, chopped
> 4 tablespoons all-purpose flour
> 1 teaspoon salt
> ½ teaspoon white pepper
> 1 cup chicken broth
> 1½ cups milk
> 2¼ teaspoons curry powder
> 4 cups cooked, shredded chicken

In a heavy-bottomed saucepan over medium heat, melt butter. Add mushrooms and onion and cook until onion is translucent, about 3 minutes.

Stir in flour, salt, and pepper and cook until bubbly. Stir in chicken broth and bring to a simmer, stirring until thickened. Add milk and curry powder and continue stirring until smooth. Stir in chicken and mix well. Turn heat to low and keep warm until ready to serve.

Serves 8

CHICKEN CURRY BUFFET

Here is a classic Bush family buffet. The buffet line starts with rice to be topped with curried chicken. Diners choose the other condiments as desired and add them to their plates as they go through the line. This serves 8.

4 cups cooked rice
Chicken Curry (page 113)
1 cup mango chutney
1 cup chopped peanuts
4 hard-cooked eggs, whites and yolks separated and mashed
4 avocados, seeded, peeled, and diced
8 slices bacon, cooked and chopped
1 cup chopped celery
1 large onion, chopped
1 cup raisins, chopped
1 cup shredded coconut, toasted
2 medium tomatoes, chopped
4 chopped serrano chiles (optional)

MEAT

Beef and Pea Pods

Mongolian Beef

Serve this dish over steamed or fried rice, or over soft noodles or fried rice noodles.

FOR MARINADE

1 teaspoon rice wine or dry sherry
1 tablespoon soy sauce
1 tablespoon vegetable oil
1 teaspoon sesame oil
¼ teaspoon baking soda
1 teaspoon cornstarch
½ teaspoon sugar
⅔ pound flank steak, sliced across grain
         on an angle into thin 3-inch strips

FOR SEASONING SAUCE

1 tablespoon hoisin sauce
1 tablespoon hot bean sauce
1 teaspoon cornstarch
½ cup water

President (41) and Mrs. Bush love Asian cuisine. When friends are invited for dinner, they don't hesitate to request Asian food.

Asian table service always includes three or more entrées. I usually prepare one dish that calls for beef as the main ingredient, one dish with pork, another with seafood, and a fourth with chicken. Bowls of steamed rice and a platter of egg rolls complete the setup. All are presented on the table, and diners help themselves family style. So keep that in mind as you plan a meal of Asian dishes throughout the book, which are some of the President and Mrs. Bush's favorites.

5 tablespoons vegetable oil
8–10 scallions, cut into 1½-inch lengths

For marinade: In a large bowl, combine rice wine, soy sauce, vegetable oil, sesame oil, baking soda, cornstarch, and sugar. Add beef strips and toss to coat. Marinate for 1 hour.

For seasoning sauce: In a bowl, combine hoisin sauce, hot bean sauce, cornstarch, and water. Set aside.

To finish: In a wok over high heat, heat vegetable oil. Stir-fry marinated beef until very lightly browned, about 1 minute. Remove with slotted spoon; set aside.

Pour off all but 2 tablespoons oil. Reheat oil in wok and add seasoning sauce. Bring to a boil. Return beef to wok and add scallions. Stir-fry for 30 seconds.

Serves 4

Beef and Pea Pods

FOR MARINADE

2 tablespoons vegetable oil
1 tablespoon rice wine or dry sherry
1 tablespoon soy sauce
½ teaspoon minced fresh ginger
¼ teaspoon sugar
½ teaspoon baking soda
1 teaspoon cornstarch
⅔ pound flank steak, sliced across the grain
on an angle into thin 3-inch strips

FOR SEASONING SAUCE

¼ cup chicken broth
½ teaspoon cornstarch
2 tablespoons water
1 tablespoon soy sauce
1 teaspoon sesame oil

TO FINISH

1 cup vegetable oil
1 garlic clove, crushed
½ pound snow peas, blanched
¼ teaspoon sugar
¼ teaspoon salt

For marinade: In a large bowl, combine oil, rice wine, soy sauce, ginger, sugar, baking soda, and cornstarch. Stir until smooth. Stir in beef strips and marinate 30 minutes.

For seasoning sauce: In a bowl, combine broth, cornstarch, water, soy sauce, and sesame oil. Stir until smooth. Set aside.

To finish: In a wok over medium heat, heat oil until smoking. Stir-fry marinated beef until very lightly browned. Remove with slotted spoon, draining well over wok; set aside.

Pour off oil into heatproof bowl. Reserve. Return 2 tablespoons to wok over high heat. Heat oil 30 seconds, then stir-fry garlic for 10 seconds and remove from wok with slotted spoon. Discard garlic. Add blanched snow peas, sugar, and salt; stir-fry for 10 seconds. Remove peas from wok with slotted spoon and arrange on a platter.

Reduce heat to medium. Add 2 tablespoons reserved oil and seasoning sauce to oil left in wok. Stir until sauce thickens slightly. Add cooked beef strips. Mix well with sauce and spoon over snow peas. Serve hot.

Serves 4

Beef Pepper Steak

Serve with white rice.

FOR MARINADE

3 tablespoons dark soy sauce
2 tablespoons plus ¾ teaspoon dry sherry
1 teaspoon salt
1½ teaspoons sugar
1½ tablespoons cornstarch
2 teaspoons sesame oil
1½ pounds flank steak, sliced across the grain
      on an angle into thin 3-inch strips

TO FINISH

4 tablespoons vegetable oil
5 slices fresh ginger
4 green bell peppers, seeded and cut
      into thin strips
2 scallions, finely chopped

For marinade: In a bowl combine soy sauce, sherry, salt, sugar, cornstarch, and sesame oil. Add beef and marinate for 15 minutes.

To finish: In a wok over high heat, heat 2 tablespoons oil until smoking and stir-fry beef quickly until meat loses its pink color. Remove beef with slotted spoon and set aside; keep warm.

Reheat wok, add 2 tablespoons oil, and stir-fry ginger slices for 30 seconds. Drain ginger slices over wok, then discard. Add bell peppers to wok and stir-fry for 1 minute, stirring well to absorb ginger-oil flavor.

Return beef to wok and stir-fry until meat is warm and the peppers are crisp-tender, about 1 minute. Remove from heat and stir in scallions.

Serves 8

Sesame Beef

1½ teaspoons sugar
3 tablespoons dark soy sauce
1 teaspoon cornstarch
¼ teaspoon pepper
1 tablespoon sesame oil
1½ pounds flank steak, sliced across the grain
      on an angle into thin 3-inch strips
1½ tablespoons sesame seeds
1½ tablespoons vegetable oil
3 garlic cloves, minced
3 scallions, finely chopped

In a bowl, combine sugar, soy sauce, cornstarch, pepper, and sesame oil. Add beef strips and toss to coat well. Marinate for 20 minutes.

Heat wok over medium heat and dry-roast sesame seeds until lightly browned. Remove to a plate and set aside.

Heat wok over high heat until just smoking, add vegetable oil and swirl to coat sides; add garlic and beef and stir-fry until beef is no longer pink, about 3 minutes.

Sprinkle with sesame seeds and remove to serving platter. Garnish with scallions.

Serves 8

Mandarin Orange Beef

½ cup rice wine
½ cup soy sauce
1½ pounds beef tenderloin, cut across the grain into thin 2-inch strips
3 tablespoons canola oil
1 cup chicken broth
4 star anise
1 tablespoon finely chopped fresh ginger
⅛ teaspoon ground cloves
2 scallions, chopped, plus 3 scallions, sliced diagonally, for garnish
1 tablespoon sugar
¼ cup rice or cider vinegar
5 dried hot red peppers
Peel of 3 mandarin oranges, thinly sliced
1 teaspoon salt
1½ teaspoons Chinese 5-spice powder

In a bowl, combine rice wine and soy sauce. Stir in beef slices and coat well.

In a wok over high heat, heat oil until smoking. Stir-fry marinated beef slices until all liquid evaporates from beef.

Add broth, star anise, ginger, cloves, chopped scallions, sugar, vinegar, dried hot red peppers, orange peel, salt, and 5-spice powder. Stir-fry until sauce reduces and thickens, coating beef and orange peel. Remove hot peppers. Garnish with sliced scallions. Serve hot.

Serves 6–8

Marinated Beef Tenderloin

I often serve this with Fabulous Noodle Kugel (page 124).

1 cup red wine
¼ cup lemon juice
½ cup soy sauce
½ cup vegetable oil
½ cup brown sugar
1 tablespoon minced ginger
3 tablespoons minced garlic
2 teaspoons dry mustard
½ teaspoon salt
¼ teaspoon pepper
3 pounds beef tenderloin, trimmed

Here the Marinated Beef Tenderloin is sliced ¼ inch thick to be served with larger than golf ball–sized Homemade Philippine Rolls (page 234) or Buttermilk Biscuits or Sour Cream Biscuits (page 226) as buffet entrées.

In a bowl, combine wine, lemon juice, soy sauce, oil, brown sugar, ginger, garlic, mustard, salt, and pepper. Add beef and marinate for at least 3 hours in refrigerator, turning beef in marinade several times.

Prepare a charcoal or gas grill and grill beef to desired doneness. Allow tenderloin to rest 20 minutes before slicing.

Serves 6–8

Fabulous Noodle Kugel

1 cup sugar
¼ teaspoon salt
1 tablespoon ground cinnamon
2 cups finely shredded peeled Granny Smith apples
7 large eggs, lightly beaten
1 pint sour cream
3 cups whole milk
1½ teaspoons vanilla extract
1 cup golden raisins
1 pound large curd cottage cheese
1 pound broad noodles
Cornflakes, crushed
4 tablespoons unsalted butter, melted

Fabulous Noodle Kugel is a recipe Mrs. Bush brought home from Las Vegas. Mrs. Elaine Wynn, wife of Steve Wynn, owner/builder of many Las Vegas casinos, hotels, and resorts, gave this recipe to her. Mrs. Bush thinks the recipe is great when served during brunch meals or as a side dish to complement beef tenderloin or roast leg of lamb.

Mr. and Mrs. Bush's granddaughter Lauren Bush, now a professional fashion model, is a vegetarian, and she rewards me with a sweet smile each time I prepare this kugel when she visits her grandparents.

In a bowl, combine sugar, salt, cinnamon, and apples. Stir in eggs. Blend in sour cream, milk, and vanilla. Stir in raisins. Fold in cottage cheese.

In a large pot of boiling water over high heat, boil noodles until al dente. Drain. Allow noodles to cool off slightly before tossing with cottage cheese mixture. Pour into large shallow Pyrex dish coated with pan spray, and level top with rubber spatula. Cover with plastic wrap and refrigerate for at least 3 hours or overnight.

Heat oven to 350°. When ready to bake, cover casserole with crushed cornflakes and drizzle with melted butter. Bake until bubbly, about 1 hour and 15 minutes. Serve hot or warm.

Serves 12–16

In the summer of 2000, former President George Bush and Mrs. Barbara Bush decided to greet the motorcade arrival of President George W. Bush for his first visit to Walker's Point as the newly inaugurated President. The First Lady, Laura, twins Jenna and Barbara, and the President's youngest brother, Marvin, along with the President's entourage were met with screams and cheers. Signs that read, "#41 Has Killed the Fatted Calf for You #43" were put together by the office staff, household staff, and family members.

Standing from left to right: Pierce Bush, Doro Koch, Brooke Sheldon, Alicia Huizar, Catie Hinkley, Paula Rendon, Jim Appleby, Jean Becker, and Tom Frechette.

Sitting: Jebby Bush, dogs Griffin and Sadie, Alina Gonzalez, Sam LeBlond, Ellie LeBlond, Gigi Koch, President #41, Mrs. Barbara Bush, Robert Koch, and me, Ariel.

Meat Sauce

3 pounds ground beef chuck
3 pounds ground beef sirloin
1 large Spanish onion, chopped
1 cup Taco Seasoning Mix (page 128)
1 cup water, or as needed

Everyone, young and old, anticipates Taco Day—for there's a rivalry among cousins. Who can devour the most tacos? The record so far is twelve, and there is a toss-up who really set the record between Sam LeBlond, Jebby Bush, Pierce Bush, or Robert Koch. None of the four grandsons wishes to yield, so we'll see what happens on the next Taco Day!

Pictured from left to right: Robert Koch, Walker Bush, Gigi Koch, Sam LeBlond, Jebby's friend Magda, Jebby, and Mrs. Barbara Bush.

In a large heavy-bottomed stockpot over medium heat, cook ground meat, stirring often, until tender and broken up and no pink remains. Drain grease. Add onion, Taco Seasoning Mix, and 1 cup water. Simmer, stirring often, for 20 minutes. Add more water as needed to keep meat mixture moist.

Makes enough to fill 48 tacos

Note: Leftover meat sauce keeps well in the freezer. Simply reheat slowly over low heat to use for same purpose or for another entrée such as chili (with or without beans) or with Velveeta cheese as an appetizer.

TACO DAY

This is the most popular get-together dish in the Bush household, and plates resemble a mountain by the time the family reaches the end of the buffet line.

To re-create your own Taco Day, set up a buffet, with dishes arranged in the following order. Be prepared: these recipes serve a crowd!

Homemade Flour Tortillas (page 128)
Crisp taco shells, heated
Meat Sauce (page 126), in a chafing dish, to keep it hot
3 cans refried beans, heated
1 head iceberg lettuce, shredded
1 pint sour cream
2 large onions, chopped
3 large ripe tomatoes, chopped
Pico de Gallo (page 129)
Walker's Point Guacamole (page 130)
Shredded Cheddar cheese
Walker's Point Tomatillo Salsa (page 130)
Walker's Point Red Salsa (page 131)

Taco Seasoning Mix

    ½ cup dried minced onions
    3 tablespoons cornstarch
    ½ cup chili powder
    3 tablespoons ground cumin
    1 tablespoon dried oregano
    2 tablespoons garlic powder
    1 tablespoon instant beef bouillon granules
    2 tablespoons cayenne pepper

Mix onions, cornstarch, chili powder, cumin, oregano, garlic powder, beef granules, and cayenne.

Makes about 1⅓ cups

Note: This may be made in advance and stored in an airtight container in refrigerator. Three tablespoons is the equivalent of 1 envelope commercial taco seasoning.

Homemade Flour Tortillas

Paula Rendon—who has been with the Bush family for more than forty-three years—once repeated the old wives' tale that Mexican girls are not permitted to marry until they show their parents they can roll a perfectly round tortilla. It was this story that encouraged the Bushes' granddaughters to help out in rolling tortillas, taking turns with the rolling pin. One can always tell they helped because of the weird-looking flour tortillas. Most, if not all, are shaped like the state of Texas—not a single round tortilla in sight! No complaints from their parents since, Paula claims, none of them learned the trick either. Just the same, these tortillas taste great.

    6 cups all-purpose flour
    1 teaspoon salt
    ½ teaspoon baking powder
    ½ cup vegetable shortening
    ½ cup hot water

In a large bowl, combine flour, salt, and baking powder. Cut in shortening until mixture resembles cornmeal. Add hot water and knead dough until well incorporated and smooth, about 3 minutes. Cover with plastic and allow dough to rest at least 30 minutes at room temperature.

Divide dough into 30 to 36 balls, about the size of golf balls. On a well-floured surface, roll as thin as you can without tearing. Dust generously with extra flour as you roll tortillas.

Cook on hot griddle, flipping once, until bubbly with brown spots on both sides.

Makes 30–36

Pico de Gallo

> 3 cups seeded and diced ripe tomatoes
> 2 cups diced red onion
> 5 tablespoons vegetable oil
> Juice of 2 limes
> 4 serrano chiles, seeded and minced
> 3 tablespoons minced cilantro
> 2 tablespoons tomato juice
> 1/4 teaspoon salt
> 1/8 teaspoon pepper
> 1/8 teaspoon garlic salt

In a large bowl, gently mix tomatoes, onion, oil, lime juice, chiles, cilantro, tomato juice, and seasonings.

Cover and refrigerate until ready to use.

Makes about 6 cups

Walker's Point Guacamole

½ cup diced red onion
3 tablespoons lime juice
2 large shallots, minced
2 teaspoons minced garlic
6 large ripe avocados, pitted and peeled
⅔ cup sour cream
4 scallions, chopped
Tabasco sauce
1 teaspoon salt
¼ teaspoon pepper
¼ cup chopped mint
1 teaspoon dried marjoram
4 tablespoons pumpkin seeds, toasted and finely chopped
6 tablespoons chopped basil
Mint sprigs, for serving

In a medium bowl, mix onion, lime juice, shallots, and garlic together. Let stand for 5 minutes.

Add avocados and mash with fork. Add sour cream and scallions. Add Tabasco to desired spiciness; add salt and pepper.

Finish by gently folding in mint, marjoram, pumpkin seeds, and basil. Transfer to serving bowl. Cover tightly with plastic wrap and refrigerate until ready to serve. Garnish with fresh mint sprigs.

Makes about 6 cups

Walker's Point Tomatillo Salsa

You may also serve salsa along with corn chip scoops or tortilla chips as an appetizer or as a sauce to complement broiled meat.

4 cups water
10 large tomatillos, husked

8 large serrano chiles
4 garlic cloves, chopped
½ teaspoon salt
1 bunch fresh cilantro
1 large Vidalia or other sweet onion,
    diced

In a large saucepan over high heat, boil water. Add tomatillos and chiles and boil together until tender. Remove from heat and allow to cool completely.

In a blender, process garlic until finely minced. Using a slotted spoon, transfer cooked tomatillos and chiles to blender. Reserve water. Add salt and pulse until mixture is chunky.

Thoroughly wash cilantro. Remove and discard large stems and wilted leaves and add cilantro to blender. Pulse repeatedly to chop coarsely, about 1 minute, or just enough to blend all ingredients. Add more salt if needed. Add poaching liquid to salsa, if needed, for thinner and spreadable consistency. Transfer to a large bowl. Stir in onion.

Refrigerate until ready to serve. Stir well before serving.

Makes 8 cups

Walker's Point Red Salsa

This is also great as a dip for chips or topping for omelets.

1 bunch fresh cilantro
4 large serrano chiles, minced
3 garlic cloves, minced
1 teaspoon salt
10 medium red tomatoes, chopped
1 large Vidalia or other sweet onion, chopped
1 (5.5-ounce) can tomato juice or V8

Thoroughly wash cilantro; remove large stems and discard wilted leaves. Using a vegetable spinner if available, spin-dry cilantro, or wrap in absorbent paper towels and press down to absorb water from leaves. Chop finely and add to large bowl with minced chiles.

Place garlic cloves on a cutting board and sprinkle with salt. Crush garlic cloves with the flat side of a knife, using salt to grind garlic into pulp. Chop with knife until finely minced. Scrape minced garlic with knife and transfer to bowl with minced chiles and cilantro. Add tomatoes and onion to bowl. Use just enough tomato juice to moisten chunky salsa. Stir to blend well. Chill in refrigerator for at least 30 minutes.

Makes about 5 cups

Here's how I set up the buffet when Beef Fajitas are on the menu for a family gathering.

Homemade Flour Tortillas (page 128)
Beef Fajitas (page 133)
3 cans refried beans, heated
1 head iceberg lettuce, shredded
1 pint sour cream
2 large onions, chopped
3 large ripe tomatoes, chopped
Pico de Gallo (page 129)
Walker's Point Guacamole (page 130)
Shredded Cheddar cheese
Walker's Point Tomatillo Salsa (page 130)
Walker's Point Red Salsa (page 131)

Beef Fajitas

This dish is another favorite for the buffet table when family and friends get together for lunch at Walker's Point in Kennebunkport, Maine.

1 can regular beer
2 tablespoons liquid smoke
1 teaspoon salt
½ teaspoon pepper
1 teaspoon garlic powder
1 teaspoon ground cumin
½ teaspoon cayenne pepper
1 teaspoon chili powder
2 (3-pound) flank steaks
2 tablespoons vegetable oil
3 medium green bell peppers, seeded and cut into strips
3 large onions, sliced

In a large bowl, combine beer, liquid smoke, salt, pepper, garlic powder, cumin, cayenne, and chili powder. Add the flank steaks and marinate in the refrigerator for at least 3 hours, turning the meat in the marinade a few times.

Prepare a charcoal or gas grill. Grill flank steaks to desired doneness (medium rare to medium). Allow the steaks to rest for at least 10 minutes before carving across the grain on an angle into thin slices.

In a large skillet over medium heat, heat the oil. Add the bell peppers and onions and cook until just tender. Add sliced beef and toss to combine. Serve as the centerpiece of a fajita buffet.

Serves 12–20

Pork Adobo

Adobo is a very popular dish from the Republic of the Philippines. The dish is aromatic and mouth-watering during and after the cooking process. A Philippine buffet will always offer this dish as one of the many entrées. To Filipinos, the absence of this dish on a buffet line is a sin. Serve with steamed rice.

2½–3 pounds pork butt
½ cup rice vinegar or cider vinegar
¼ cup soy sauce
10–15 black peppercorns, cracked
6 garlic cloves, crushed
2 bay leaves
2 teaspoons cornstarch
1 teaspoon sugar
1 tablespoon water

Cut pork butt into large chunks; trim excess fat and discard. Rinse pork chunks in running cold water and transfer pieces directly to a large heavy-bottomed saucepan. Add vinegar, soy sauce, cracked black peppercorns, and garlic. Toss to coat all meat pieces. Add bay leaves. Simmer for 25 minutes or until seasoning sauce is reduced by half and bubbly. Remove saucepan from heat. Discard bay leaves.

In a small bowl, combine cornstarch, sugar, and water to make a paste. Stir into pork. Return saucepan to heat and simmer for 10 minutes.

Serves 4

VARIATION

Pork Spareribs Adobo: Follow Pork Adobo recipe, substituting pork spareribs (cut across bones to make smaller pieces) for the pork butt. Simmer for at least 45 minutes to ensure meat is done and liquid is reduced to a thick sauce. Skim off and discard grease and bay leaves.

Pork Chops Adobo

4 thick pork chops, bone in
Salt and pepper
2 tablespoons all-purpose flour
8 tablespoons (1 stick) unsalted butter
6 garlic cloves, crushed
½ cup cider vinegar
¼ cup soy sauce
10–15 black peppercorns, cracked
2 tablespoons cornstarch
1 tablespoon sugar
1 tablespoon water

Heat oven to 375°.

Season pork chops with salt and pepper. Dust with flour.

In a saucepan over medium heat, heat 4 tablespoons butter. Cook chops until light golden brown, about 2 minutes per side. Transfer chops to a baking pan and set aside.

Scrape burnt sediments from saucepan and add garlic and cook until fragrant; add vinegar, soy sauce, and cracked black peppercorns and boil, stirring constantly, until liquid is reduced by half and bubbly.

In a small bowl, combine cornstarch, sugar, and water to make a paste. Add to saucepan. Cook sauce, stirring for 2 minutes, or until thickened. Add remaining 4 tablespoons butter. Stir to blend well. Generously brush pork chops with hot sauce. Bake for 40 minutes, basting with sauce during baking process until all sauce has been used.

Serves 4

Sweet-and-Sour Pork

FOR MARINADE

1½ pounds pork tenderloin,
    cut into cubes
1 teaspoon salt
3 tablespoons soy sauce
2 tablespoons cornstarch
2 tablespoons water
6 cups vegetable oil

FOR BATTER

¾ cup all-purpose flour
½ cup cornstarch
1 cup ice water
2 large eggs

FOR VEGETABLES

1 green bell pepper, seeded and cut
    into 1-inch pieces
1 red bell pepper, seeded and cut
    into 1-inch pieces
2 medium carrots, sliced
¼ cup water chestnuts
8 slices canned pineapple, cut into 1-inch chunks

FOR SAUCE

1 tablespoon vegetable oil
1 garlic clove, finely minced
½ cup chicken broth
½ cup ketchup
2 tablespoons rice vinegar
1 cup sugar
Pinch of ground cloves
2 teaspoons cornstarch
½ cup water
¼ cup whole almonds, toasted

For marinade: With the flat side of a cleaver, pound pork gently to flatten cubes.

In a bowl, combine salt, soy sauce, cornstarch, and water; add pork and marinate for 30 minutes.

In a wok heat oil to 350º.

For batter: In a bowl, combine flour, cornstarch, ice water, and eggs. Drain pork from marinade. Coat each piece of marinated pork with batter. Slowly lower coated pork into hot oil. Deep-fry for 3 minutes, or until browned. Remove pork from oil with slotted spoon and transfer to a bowl.

Turn heat up to high and heat oil to 400º. Carefully place pork all at once in hot oil and deep-fry again for about 30 seconds until crisp. Remove again with slotted spoon, draining well over wok; place pork on a platter.

For vegetables: Pour off all but 2 tablespoons oil. Reduce heat to medium. Add peppers, carrots, water chestnuts, and pineapple; stir-fry for 1 minute. Remove from heat and set aside.

For sauce: In a small sauccpan over medium-high heat, heat oil. Add garlic and cook 1 minute, or until golden brown. Stir in broth, ketchup, vinegar, sugar, and cloves and bring to a boil.

In a measuring cup, dissolve cornstarch in water. Stir into sauce and cook, stirring, until sauce has thickened. Remove from heat.

Add pork and almonds to vegetables in wok. Pour in sauce and toss to coat well. Serve immediately.

Serves 8

Taiwanese Barbecued Pork

2 tablespoons dry sherry
2 thin slices fresh ginger
1 tablespoon oyster sauce
4½ teaspoons soy sauce
2 tablespoons hoisin sauce
2 tablespoons ketchup
1½ teaspoons bean sauce
1 tablespoon sugar
½ teaspoon ground cinnamon
¼ teaspoon ground allspice
1½ pounds boneless pork shoulder
*   or butt, cut into 5 x 2-inch strips*
1 tablespoon honey
1 cucumber, sliced, for garnish

In a bowl, combine sherry, ginger, oyster sauce, soy sauce, hoisin sauce, ketchup, bean sauce, sugar, cinnamon, and allspice. Add pork and toss to coat (be careful not to tear meat). Marinate in the refrigerator for 6 hours. Remove meat and drain well. Reserve 3 tablespoons of marinade and discard remaining sauce. Mix in honey to reserved marinade and set aside.

Fill a shallow roasting pan with 1 inch of water and place in bottom of oven. Remove racks from oven. Heat oven to 350°. Spray an oven rack with pan spray and hang pork strips securely from rack. Slide rack into top position in oven (with meat hanging over drip pan) and "barbecue" pork for 30 minutes. Slide rack out carefully and baste meat with honey mixture. Roast for 15 minutes; baste again. Roast for another 10 minutes, until pork is crisp and golden brown.

Remove from oven and allow pork to cool. Cut on diagonal into ¼-inch slices and arrange in overlapping layers on a platter. Garnish with cucumber slices.

Serves 4

Marinated Pork with Scallions

FOR MARINADE

1 teaspoon rice wine or dry sherry
½ teaspoon minced fresh ginger
½ teaspoon salt
1 teaspoon cornstarch
⅔ pound pork shoulder or butt,
    cut into 1 x ½-inch strips

FOR SEASONING SAUCE

½ cup water
2 teaspoons cornstarch
¼ cup chicken broth
½ teaspoon salt

TO FINISH

1 cup vegetable oil
3 cups sliced scallions

For marinade: In a bowl, combine rice wine, ginger, salt, and cornstarch. Add pork strips and toss well. Marinate for 30 minutes.

For seasoning sauce: In a bowl, mix water, cornstarch, chicken broth, and salt. Set aside.

To finish: In a wok over medium heat, heat oil until it starts to smoke. Stir-fry marinated pork until very lightly browned. Remove pork with slotted spoon, draining over wok.

Pour off all but 2 tablespoons oil. Add scallions and stir-fry for 1 minute. Add seasoning sauce to wok; stir-fry until sauce thickens slightly. Stir in pork. Serve hot.

Serves 4

Crispy Pork

FOR MARINADE

2 egg whites, beaten
1 tablespoon cornstarch
⅓ teaspoon salt
1 pound lean pork loin, cut into
        2 x ¼-inch strips

1 cup peanut oil
1½ tablespoons vegetable oil
3 garlic cloves, minced
1½ tablespoons fresh minced ginger
2 scallions, minced
3 tablespoons dark soy sauce
1½ tablespoons cider vinegar
1½ tablespoons chili bean paste
1½ tablespoons sesame oil
1 tablespoon sugar
1½ tablespoons dry sherry

For marinade: In a bowl, combine egg whites, cornstarch, and salt. Add pork strips and toss to coat evenly. Marinate for at least 15 minutes.

In a wok over high heat, heat peanut oil until smoking. Add the pork, stirring constantly to keep pork from sticking. When meat turns white, drain well with a slotted spoon over wok and set aside.

Discard peanut oil. Wipe wok clean; reheat until smoking. Add vegetable oil, garlic, ginger, and scallions; stir-fry for 30 seconds. Add soy sauce, vinegar, bean paste, sesame oil, sugar, and sherry. Bring to a boil. Return cooked meat to wok and stir-fry for 2 minutes, tossing to coat meat well with the sauce.

Serves 4

Marinated Pork Tenderloin with Mustard Sauce

FOR MARINADE

¼ *cup soy sauce*
¼ *cup bourbon*
2 *tablespoons brown sugar*
3 *pounds pork tenderloin*

FOR MUSTARD SAUCE

⅓ *cup sour cream*
⅓ *cup mayonnaise*
½ *cup Dijon-style mustard*
1 *tablespoon finely chopped scallions*
1½ *teaspoons rice or cider vinegar*
Salt

For marinade: In a bowl, combine soy sauce, bourbon, and brown sugar. Set pork tenderloin in a shallow pan, pour in marinade, and marinate at room temperature for 2 hours, turning occasionally.

Heat oven to 325º.

Remove pork from marinade and transfer to baking sheet. Bake, basting frequently with marinade, for 1 hour, or until tender.

For mustard sauce: In a bowl, mix together sour cream, mayonnaise, mustard, scallions, vinegar, and salt to taste; blend well. Serve cold or slightly heated.

Cut tenderloin on the diagonal into thin slices. Serve with mustard sauce.

Serves 6

Curry-Glazed Pork Chops

2 tablespoons olive oil
1 large onion, chopped
2 tablespoons all-purpose flour
2 tablespoons brown sugar
1 tablespoon curry powder
1 teaspoon salt
1 teaspoon ground cinnamon
1 beef bouillon cube
1 cup water
2 tablespoons ketchup
1 tablespoon applesauce
1 tablespoon apricot preserves
4 thick pork chops, bone in

Heat oven to 400º. Spray a baking dish with pan spray.

In a saucepan over medium-high heat, heat oil. Add onion and cook until translucent. Blend in flour, brown sugar, curry powder, salt, and cinnamon. Add bouillon cube, water, ketchup, applesauce, and apricot preserves and bring to a boil. Reduce heat and allow glaze to simmer for 5 minutes.

Dip pork chops, one at a time, into glaze to coat well and arrange on a baking dish. Reserve rest of glaze. Bake pork chops for 20 minutes. Spoon remaining glaze over pork chops and bake for 20 more minutes.

Serves 4

Peking Spareribs

Ask your favorite butcher to cut the spareribs in half lengthwise.

FOR MARINADE

2 pounds baby back spareribs
1 teaspoon dry sherry
1 teaspoon minced fresh ginger
1 tablespoon soy sauce
½ teaspoon baking soda
1 tablespoon cornstarch
1 tablespoon all-purpose flour
1 tablespoon ice water

FOR SEASONING SAUCE

1 tablespoon Worcestershire sauce
1 tablespoon ketchup
1 tablespoon sugar
1 teaspoon ground cinnamon
2 tablespoons water
½ teaspoon cornstarch

TO FINISH

5 cups vegetable oil
Parsley, for garnish
Sliced pineapple, for garnish
Steamed rice, for serving

For marinade: Cut between ribs to make 2-inch pieces.

In a bowl, combine sherry, ginger, soy sauce, baking soda, cornstarch, flour, and ice water. Add ribs and marinate in the refrigerator for 4 hours, turning the ribs in the marinade a few times.

For seasoning sauce: In a bowl, combine Worcestershire, ketchup, sugar, cinnamon, water, and cornstarch. Set aside.

To finish: In a wok over high heat, heat oil to 350º. Carefully lower ribs into oil and deep-fry for about 3 minutes, until crisp and lightly browned. Remove with slotted spoon, draining well. Set aside.

Pour off all but 2 tablespoons oil. Heat oil for 30 seconds, then add seasoning sauce. Bring to a boil, stirring occasionally. Add ribs and toss to coat well. Transfer to platter and garnish with parsley and pineapple. Serve with steamed rice.

Serves 4

Walker's Point Shish Kebabs

FOR MARINADE

1½ cups olive oil
¾ cup soy sauce
¼ cup Worcestershire sauce
2 tablespoons dry mustard
2½ teaspoons salt
1 tablespoon black pepper
1 tablespoon crushed dried rosemary
½ cup wine vinegar
1½ teaspoons dried parsley
2 garlic cloves, crushed
½ cup lemon juice
2 pounds boneless lamb shoulder, cut into 16 cubes

1–2 zucchini, cut into 8 (¾-inch) rings
1–2 yellow squash, cut into 8 (¾-inch) rings
1 red bell pepper, seeded and cut into 8 (1½-inch) squares
8 small white onions
8 mushrooms

For marinade: In a blender, combine oil, soy sauce, Worcestershire, mustard, salt, pepper, rosemary, vinegar, parsley, garlic, and lemon juice. Process until thick and smooth.

Pour marinade over lamb cubes and marinate overnight in refrigerator.

Prepare a charcoal or gas grill.

Skewer together each vegetable separately. Dry lamb cubes with paper towels and skewer together. Coat vegetables with pan spray and sprinkle with salt and pepper. Grill lamb and vegetables, turning often to ensure browning. Remove from skewers and arrange on plates, alternating assorted vegetables with lamb as if pieces have been skewered and grilled together.

Serves 4

Rolled Lamb Divine

Ask your favorite butcher to remove bones from a leg of lamb. Serve with Jalapeño Jelly and Spaetzle Noodles.

> 1 cup Dijon-style mustard
> 2 tablespoons chopped rosemary
> 2 tablespoons olive oil
> 2 tablespoons soy sauce
> ½ teaspoon ground ginger
> 1 (4-pound) boneless leg of lamb,
>   tied into a roll with cotton string
> Jalapeño Jelly (recipe follows), for serving
> Spaetzle Noodles (recipe follows), for serving

In a bowl, combine mustard, rosemary, oil, soy sauce, and ginger. Generously brush rolled lamb with mixture, coating all sides. Marinate in refrigerator for at least 6 hours.

Heat oven to 350º.

Transfer lamb to roasting pan and roast 1 hour. Reduce temperature to 225º and roast for another 15 minutes. Let rest for 20 minutes before carving.

Serves 12

Jalapeño Jelly

> 9 large fresh jalapeños, chopped
> 1 large green bell pepper, seeded and chopped
> 5 cups sugar
> ¾ cup apple cider vinegar
> 1 (3-ounce) bottle liquid fruit pectin

In a large saucepan, combine jalapeños, bell pepper, sugar, and vinegar. Bring to a boil. Boil, uncovered, for 5 minutes. Remove saucepan from heat and cool for 30 minutes.

Skim off any foam that rises. Add fruit pectin. Mix well; bring to a full rolling boil a second time. The jelly has a tendency to boil over, so stir constantly for 10 minutes. Lift saucepan off heat if jelly is boiling over and return to heat only when mixture subsides. Remove from heat. Place saucepan directly over larger bowl of ice water and stir continuously for 6 more minutes to cool. Skim off any foam. Carefully pour hot mixture into 4 (1-pint) sterilized jelly jars. Do not place lids on jars until fully cooled off.

Makes 4 pints

Spaetzle Noodles

Chef Frank Ruta, one of the outstanding chefs at the White House during Mr. Bush's presidential tenure, showed me how to prepare this dish. I took the partially prepared product up to Camp David to finish the process and serve to President and Mrs. Bush as a side dish. Don Johnson and Melanie Griffith were guests at Camp David at the time.

> 4 large eggs
> ⅓ cup chicken broth
> 1½ tablespoons unsalted butter, melted
> ¾ cup all-purpose flour
> ½ cup clarified butter
> Bacon bits or chopped parsley, for garnish

In a bowl, combine eggs, chicken broth, butter, and flour. Beat with electric mixer at medium speed for 7 minutes. Batter should have a runny consistency.

In a 10-quart pot, bring salted water to a boil. Thinly and evenly spread batter on a wooden board. Slightly tilt board over pot and, using a flat knife, scrape thin strings of batter into simmering water. Cook until noodles float to the surface. Scoop noodles out and transfer to a bowl with ice water. When cool, transfer to a colander and drain. This may be prepared a day ahead.

At serving time, sauté noodles in clarified butter until noodles begin to brown and puff. Sprinkle with crispy bacon bits or parsley.

Serves 6

Saudi Arabian Prince Bandar's conquest of the Walker's Point kitchen

PRINCE BANDAR'S KAPSA, MARAK, AND SALSA

During his second visit to Walker's Point on June 26, 1998, Prince Bandar of Saudi Arabia surprised everyone by saying that he would cook lunch for the former President and First Lady.

Sure enough, His Highness's entourage drove in the next day with two ice chests full of food, each ingredient and condiment specially prepared and packed separately. His Highness claimed this dish is a favorite of most desert travelers simply because it can be prepared effortlessly around campfires, thrown together in a large pot, and consumed while on the move. His Highness also called this meal "bachelor's dish." It was the most memorable, fun-filled event I had ever experienced in any kitchen, with lots of chuckling and laughter.

Prepare a potful today for dinner and tomorrow's lunch—and dinner and lunch the next day. The Kapsa, Marak, and Salsa served together will serve 20 generously.

Kapsa

1 cup (2 sticks) unsalted butter
2 medium onions, chopped
2 cups chopped tomatoes
1½ pounds lamb loin, cut into large chunks
1 tablespoon pepper
2 tablespoons ground cumin
2 tablespoons lime powder (see Note)
4 cups chicken broth
3 dehydrated whole limes (see Note)
2 large eggplants, cut into large chunks
1 cup tomato paste
2 cups tomato sauce
Salt and pepper
4 cups basmati rice

In a large heavy pot over medium heat, melt butter. Add onions and cook until soft and tender. Stir in tomatoes and lamb; cook until lamb is no longer pink. Stir in pepper, cumin, and lime powder and simmer for 5 minutes. Add chicken broth, whole limes, eggplant, tomato paste, and tomato sauce and simmer for 30 minutes. Season mixture with salt and pepper. When eggplant is tender, add basmati rice and continue simmering until rice turns fluffy.

Serves 12

Note: Lime powder and dehydrated limes are available in Middle Eastern markets.

Marak

6 tablespoons corn oil
2 cups finely chopped onion
2 cups chopped tomatoes
1½ pounds lamb loin, cut into large chunks
1 teaspoon black pepper
2 tablespoons ground cumin
2 tablespoons lime powder (see Note)
3 cups beef broth
1 large eggplant, cut into large chunks
2 large potatoes, cut into large chunks
2 jalapeños, cut into halves
12 long beans, cut into 2-inch lengths
3 dehydrated whole limes (see Note)
1 cup tomato paste
2 cups tomato sauce
Salt and pepper

In a large heavy pot over medium heat, heat oil. Add onion and cook until translucent. Add tomatoes and lamb chunks and cook until lamb is no longer pink. Stir in pepper, cumin, and lime powder and simmer for 5 minutes. Add beef broth, eggplant, potatoes, jalapeños, long beans, dehydrated whole limes, tomato paste, and tomato sauce and simmer for 30 minutes. Season mixture well with salt and pepper.

Serves 12

Note: Lime powder and dehydrated limes are available in Middle Eastern markets.

Salsa

This salsa is a fine complement to both Kapsa and Marak.

> 3 cups seeded chopped tomatoes
> ½ cup seeded chopped jalapeños
> 2 cups minced onion
> 1 cup fresh lemon juice
> Salt and pepper

Mix together tomatoes, jalapeños, onion, and lemon juice. Season with salt and pepper. Chill until ready to serve.

Makes about 5 cups

SEAFOOD

Poached Salmon with Dill-Mayonnaise Sauce •
Striped Bass with Walker's Point Fish Sauce • Broiled Haddock
with Mango Sauce • Spike's Marinated Swordfish • Walker's Point
Lobster Salad • Shrimp Creole • Shrimp Curry • Seafood Casserole •
Shrimp Egg Foo Yong • Seafood Newburg

Seafood Casserole

Poached Salmon with Dill-Mayonnaise Sauce

This is equally delicious—and impressive—made with rockfish or striped bass.

FOR POACHING

2 quarts water
2 cups dry white wine
2 tablespoons unsalted butter
½ cup sliced carrots
½ cup sliced celery
½ cup sliced onion
1 bay leaf
10 sprigs parsley
6 peppercorns
4 whole cloves
2 lemons
1 whole salmon (3–5 pounds)

FOR SAUCE

4 tablespoons hot water
1 envelope unflavored gelatin
1¼ cups mayonnaise
1¼ cups sour cream
2 teaspoons Worcestershire sauce
Juice of ½ lemon
2 tablespoons dried dill weed
Salt and pepper

FOR PRESENTATION

1 seedless cucumber, thinly sliced
1 pimiento-stuffed olive

For poaching: In a large pot, combine water, wine, butter, carrots, celery, onion, bay leaf, parsley, peppercorns, and cloves. Cut the lemons in half and squeeze in the juice. Add lemon halves and bring poaching mixture to a boil over high heat.

Wrap fish in cheesecloth. Secure by tying ends of cloth. Immerse in poaching mixture, reduce heat, and simmer for 1 hour. Allow extra cloth to hang over edge of pot for easy handling. Turn off heat. Remove poached fish from pot. Drain well. Allow poached fish to stand until cool enough to handle.

For sauce: Place the hot water in a small bowl. Sprinkle gelatin on top and stir to dissolve. In a bowl, combine mayonnaise, sour cream, Worcestershire, lemon juice, and dill weed. Season with salt and pepper and stir until smooth. Gradually add gelatin to mayonnaise–sour cream mixture; blend well. Chill until ready to use.

Unwrap fish. Carefully skin and bone the fish, trying not to flake fish into tiny pieces; keep fish in as large chunks as possible.

On a large serving platter, reshape fish pieces into the form of a whole fish. Press pieces tightly so they hold their shape.

For presentation: Generously coat molded fish with sauce, spreading it evenly. Arrange cucumber slices in overlapping rows, starting from end of tail, to suggest fish scales. Cut the olive in half crosswise and press onto head, cut side up, for the eyes.

Chill thoroughly before serving.

Serves 8–16, and up to 24
as part of a buffet

Striped Bass with Walker's Point Fish Sauce

FOR SAUCE

⅓ cup plus 2 teaspoons lemon juice
3 tablespoons tomato paste
2 tablespoons minced shallot
2 tablespoons minced cilantro
1 tablespoon minced pitted green olives
4 garlic cloves, minced
1 teaspoon chopped capers
4 egg yolks
1 cup (2 sticks) unsalted butter, melted
      and cooled slightly
Salt and pepper

FOR FISH

4 (8-ounce) striped bass fillets, skin on
½ teaspoon curry powder
1 teaspoon salt
½ teaspoon pepper
Dash of paprika
2 teaspoons finely chopped parsley

For sauce: In a medium bowl, mix ⅓ cup lemon juice, tomato paste, shallot, cilantro, olives, garlic, and capers. Set aside.

In top of double boiler over barely simmering water, whisk egg yolks and 2 teaspoons lemon juice until mixture begins to thicken, about 2 minutes.

Whisk in melted butter, a drop at a time, until sauce begins to thicken, and then whisk in remaining butter in slow stream. Continue whisking until sauce thickens to consistency of whipped cream. Adjust taste of sauce with salt and pepper. Fold in reserved lemon-tomato mixture. Set aside.

For fish: Heat broiler.

Arrange fillets on baking sheet. Sprinkle with curry powder, salt, pepper, paprika, and parsley.

Broil fillets for about 4 minutes, until opaque. Remove from broiler and cover with sauce. Broil for 2 minutes more. Serve hot.

Serves 4

Broiled Haddock with Mango Sauce

Just like lobster, haddock is abundant in Maine, and I don't like to skimp on it. Serve with vegetables of your choice.

FOR SAUCE

4 tablespoons unsalted butter
¼ cup all-purpose flour
¼ teaspoon salt
¼ cup light brown sugar
½ cup hot water
Juice of 2 large lemons
¼ cup chopped raisins
¼ cup peeled, seeded, and diced mango
2 teaspoons chopped parsley

FOR FISH

1 teaspoon salt
½ teaspoon pepper
1 teaspoon paprika
1 teaspoon garlic powder
6 (8-ounce) portions haddock fillet
Thin lemon slices, for garnish

For sauce: In a saucepan over medium heat, melt butter. Add flour, salt, and sugar and cook, stirring for about 3 minutes.

Combine hot water and lemon juice and add to roux in saucepan. Whisk well to blend. Cook over medium heat for 5–6 minutes, stirring often, until thick. Add raisins and reduce heat to low. Cook for another 2 minutes. Remove from heat and stir in diced mango and parsley. Set aside.

For fish: Heat broiler and coat baking sheet with pan spray.

Combine salt, pepper, paprika, and garlic powder in a small jar with lid. Shake bottle until all ingredients are combined. Place fish on baking sheet and sprinkle generously with seasoning mix. Broil fish for 8–10 minutes, or until fillets are browned and flake easily.

Transfer fish to dinner plates. Garnish each portion with lemon slices. Drizzle sauce along one side of fish.

Serves 6

Spike's Marinated Swordfish

Spike and Betsy Hemmingway are close friends of President (41) and Mrs. Bush. They have a summer residence in Kennebunkport, Maine, and spend their summers there almost at the same time as the Bush family. Spike is Doro's godfather and Sam, Doro's oldest son, is Betsy's godson. Betsy grew up in Greenwich, Connecticut, so President Bush has known her all his life; Spike grew up in Rye, New York, and Mrs. Bush has known him all her life.

> 2 cups mayonnaise
> 1/3 cup lemon juice
> 1 teaspoon salt
> 1/2 teaspoon pepper
> 1/2 teaspoon cayenne pepper
> 4 (6 to 8-ounce) swordfish steaks

In a bowl, whisk together mayonnaise, lemon juice, salt, pepper, and cayenne pepper until smooth. Coat swordfish completely with sauce and let marinate in refrigerator for at least 3 hours.

Prepare a charcoal or gas grill. Grill swordfish about 2 minutes per side. The grill will flare up, due to the oil in the mayonnaise. Don't be alarmed. The flames will die down. A lovely ivory color and light brown edges indicate doneness.

Serve right away, or keep warm in a low oven.

Serves 4

VARIATION

Replace 1 cup of the mayonnaise with 1 cup canola oil and replace the cayenne with two tablespoons Old Bay seasoning.

During my more than twenty years of service with the Bush family, I cannot recall any single visitor to Walker's Point during the summer who was not served a Maine lobster dinner—or who did not dine out on lobster with President and Mrs. Bush in one of the many fine restaurants in the beautiful town of Kennebunkport, Maine. The only excuse for missing this meal was an allergy to shellfish. Other than that, when in Maine, not devouring a lobster was and always will be a sin.

Preparing lobster meals is a walk in the park. It really is an easy task. I say this not because of my years of experience in preparing and serving the meal, but because it takes only 20 minutes to steam or boil a potful of lobsters, and a few minutes to crack the claws and clip the bellies open lengthwise or split in half completely. I simply arrange the lobsters on individual dinner plates—pre-plated with all the salads or side dishes that complement the lobster—and provide large empty bowls around the table. The guests will snap, break, poke, and dig out the lobster meat and fill the bowls with empty shells all by themselves. Keep food hot and serve it immediately. As Paula Zahn constantly and jokingly reminds everyone, "Señora wants food 'peeping' hot!"—with her intentional mispronunciation of "piping."

President Bush is a natural, down-to-earth person. When friends stop by to drop something off for him at the office, his quick reaction and kindness of heart leads to inviting them to stay for a quick bite to eat. When Mr. Bush calls the kitchen and the question is "What are we having for lunch or dinner?" I always brace myself for a heavy roll. He will always follow it up with "Can you add three more?" Or, "I invited so-and-so and there's six of them." Or, "Didn't anyone at the office inform you about the added guest for lunch?" These are his favorite lines. He knows I can handle the load, but there are times when the call comes in as close as 20 minutes before serving time, or occasionally while making head counts, I will find more in attendance than I had planned for. Talk about finding yourself in a hot spot! Thanks to a fully stocked refrigerator and freezer and the convenience of quick defrost mode in a microwave oven, I have not failed to provide yet.

If all else fails, there are reliable suppliers all around town who can quickly come to the rescue. My special thanks to The Bradbury Brothers' Market, Clam Shack and Seafood Market, Port Lobster, Patten's Berry Farm, H.B. Provisions, and the many more who have always bailed me out in my times of need.

WALKER'S POINT LOBSTER DINNER

Here is the menu for the symbolic Walker's Point lobster dinner.

1 (1½-pound) whole lobster per person, boiled or steamed
Lemon wedges
Individual cups of light olive oil mixed with lemon juice, for dipping
Broiled red bell pepper strips on lettuce beds
Baked sweet potatoes
Buttered corn on the cob
Puffed Cheese Rolls (page 231)
Pecan Pie (page 253)

Walker's Point Lobster Salad

FOR SALAD

2 heads Bibb lettuce, cut in half

16 asparagus spears, steamed

2 ripe avocados, pitted, peeled, and sliced

4 large eggs, hard-cooked and sliced
      with egg cutter

Alfalfa sprouts, rinsed and drained

FOR DRESSING

1 garlic clove, minced

1 cup mayonnaise

2 tablespoons chopped parsley

1 tablespoon ketchup

2 teaspoons drained capers

2 teaspoons spicy mustard

2 teaspoons drained prepared horseradish

1½ teaspoons chopped tarragon

½ teaspoon crumbled dried oregano

¼ teaspoon Worcestershire sauce

⅛ teaspoon cayenne pepper

Salt

FOR TOPPING

1 pound cooked lobster meat, sliced

½ cup diced celery

4 scallions, chopped

1 green bell pepper, seeded and cut
      into ¼-inch dice

2 tablespoons lemon juice

8 small cantaloupe wedges, for garnish

12 small honeydew wedges, for garnish

8 small lemon wedges, for garnish

For salad: On 4 dinner plates, arrange lettuce, asparagus, avocados, and egg slices. Top with alfalfa sprouts, shaped in rings to be filled with lobster topping. Set aside.

For dressing: In a blender or food processor, combine garlic, mayonnaise, parsley, ketchup, capers, mustard, horseradish, tarragon, oregano, Worcestershire, and cayenne pepper. Puree until smooth. Season with salt. Set aside.

For topping: In a large bowl, combine lobster, celery, scallions, and bell pepper. Mix in lemon juice and ¼ cup dressing. Chill in refrigerator until ready to serve.

Mound lobster salad in center of alfalfa rings. Drizzle a few drops of dressing on asparagus, avocados, and egg slices. Garnish each serving with 2 cantaloupe wedges, 3 honeydew wedges, and 2 lemon wedges. Pass the remaining dressing separately.

Serves 4

Shrimp Creole

2 tablespoons unsalted butter
½ cup minced onion
2 tablespoons all-purpose flour
¼ cup thinly sliced celery
1 teaspoon minced parsley
½ cup minced green bell pepper
1 bay leaf
Dash of cayenne pepper
¼ teaspoon white pepper
½ teaspoon salt
1 (6-ounce) can tomato paste
3 cups water
2 cups cooked shrimp, split in half lengthwise

In a saucepan over medium heat, melt butter. Add onion and cook until translucent. Stir in flour, then stir in celery, parsley, bell pepper, bay leaf, cayenne pepper, white pepper, salt, tomato paste, and water. Reduce heat to low and cook, stirring occasionally, until thickened. Stir in shrimp and cook for a minute or two to heat the shrimp through.

Serves 8

Shrimp Curry

This is the centerpiece of the Shrimp Curry Buffet.

8 tablespoons (1 stick) unsalted butter
2 cups chopped mushrooms
1 onion, chopped
1½ pounds medium shrimp, peeled, deveined, and cut in half lengthwise
4 tablespoons all-purpose flour
1 teaspoon salt
½ teaspoon white pepper
2 tablespoons water
1 cup chicken broth
1½ cups milk
2 tablespoons onion juice
2¼ teaspoons curry powder

SHRIMP CURRY BUFFET

The buffet starts with rice to be topped with Shrimp Curry. Diners choose which condiments are desired and add them to their plates as they move through the buffet.

6 cups cooked rice (in a chafing dish)
Shrimp Curry (in a chafing dish)
1 cup mango chutney
1 cup chopped peanuts
Chopped egg whites (from 6 hard-cooked eggs)
Crumbled egg yolks (from 6 hard-cooked eggs)
3 avocados, seeded, peeled, and diced
12 slices bacon, cooked and chopped
1 large onion, chopped
1 cup chopped raisins
1 cup shredded coconut, toasted
2 medium tomatoes, chopped
6 serrano chiles, minced (optional)

In a saucepan over medium heat, melt butter. Add mushrooms and onion and cook until onion is translucent, about 3 minutes. Add shrimp and cook for 1 minute. Remove from heat.

In a small bowl, mix flour, salt, pepper, and water into a paste and stir into shrimp mixture. Return pan to heat and bring to a simmer. Stir in chicken broth and cook, stirring, until thickened. Add milk, onion juice, and curry powder and continue stirring until smooth. Keep heated until ready to serve. Transfer to serving bowl. Serve shrimp curry along with other condiments in individual serving bowls and offer at a buffet table.

Serves 6

Seafood Casserole

Mrs. Grace Walker shared this recipe with me. It was the entrée during the inaugural brunch of Governor John Ellis Bush of Florida. It was said that the brunch was delayed a bit due to Mrs. Walker's presence in the kitchen, making sure she got the recipe from the catering chef. Somehow she succeeded in acquiring the ingredients, but no measurements or quantities were provided. I tested the recipe using my own measurements and came up with a recipe that has been frequently served to visiting friends and relatives at Walker's Point, Kennebunkport, Maine.

FOR SAUCE

4 tablespoons unsalted butter
1 small onion, chopped
2 tablespoons all-purpose flour
1 teaspoon salt
½ teaspoon paprika
Dash of cayenne pepper
2 cups chicken broth
1½ cups heavy cream
3 egg yolks
2 tablespoons dry sherry

FOR FILLING

1½ pounds asparagus
½ pound cooked crabmeat, picked over
½ pound cooked lobster tail, cut into chunks
12 cooked shrimp, peeled and split lengthwise, veins removed
½ pound sea scallops
½ pint shucked oysters, drained

FOR TOPPING

½ package bread stuffing mix
½ cup grated Parmesan cheese

Heat oven to 350°. Butter a 12 x 9-inch casserole dish.

For sauce: In a medium saucepan over medium heat, melt butter. Add onion and cook until translucent. Add flour, salt, paprika, and cayenne; stir 1 minute to blend. Gradually stir in broth and cream and continue stirring over medium heat until thick and smooth. Remove from heat.

In a small bowl, beat egg yolks with a wire whisk until pale. Add a little of the hot sauce into beaten egg yolks; whip to incorporate, then transfer this mixture to the remaining hot sauce. Return saucepan to medium heat; whisk constantly until thickened. Stir in sherry. Remove from heat and set aside.

For filling: Snap off tough parts of asparagus spears. Cut asparagus in half, 3–4 inches long. Steam asparagus until tender but firm, about 2 minutes. Layer bottom of casserole dish with asparagus and top with one-third of the sauce. Add crabmeat, lobster, shrimp, scallops, and oysters in layers. Gradually pour remaining sauce over seafood; spread evenly toward edge of dish.

For topping: Prepare stuffing according to package directions. Spread bread stuffing over seafood-cream mixture, covering mixture entirely. Sprinkle top with Parmesan cheese. Bake for 20–25 minutes, or until bubbly and golden brown.

Serves 10–12

Note: I sometimes offer the other half of the bread stuffing as a side dish if another starch (rice or noodles) is not included on the menu.

Shrimp Egg Foo Yong

FOR SAUCE

2 tablespoons cornstarch
1/4 cup cold water
2 cups chicken stock
2 tablespoons soy sauce
Sesame oil (optional)

FOR EGG FOO YONG

6 large eggs
1/2 cup diced cooked shrimp
1/4 cup chopped onion
1/4 cup sliced water chestnuts
1 cup bean sprouts, blanched
1 teaspoon soy sauce
1/2 teaspoon salt
1/8 teaspoon pepper

For sauce: In a cup, make a paste of cornstarch and water.

In a small saucepan, boil chicken stock. Remove from heat and stir cornstarch paste into stock. Return to heat and cook, stirring constantly, until clear and thickened. Add soy sauce. Add a few dashes of sesame oil, if desired. Keep hot.

For egg foo yong: In a bowl, beat eggs until very light. Blend in shrimp, onion, water chestnuts, bean sprouts, soy sauce, salt, and pepper.

Heat heavy skillet and spray with pan spray. With a 4-ounce ladle, pour batter into skillet to make a patty. When brown, flip like a pancake. Brown other side. Repeat to make 12 patties. Serve with sauce.

Serves 6

Seafood Newburg

Serve with fresh seasonal vegetables such as steamed asparagus, broccoli, or cauliflower.

FOR SEAFOOD

1 pound lobster meat, scallops, crabmeat, jumbo shrimp, or shad roe
4 tablespoons unsalted butter, melted
4 tablespoons lemon juice
4 dashes of paprika
4 pinches of Old Bay seasoning

FOR SAUCE

2 tablespoons unsalted butter
1 cup heavy cream
4 tablespoons Sauternes
½ teaspoon salt
¼ teaspoon cayenne pepper
3 egg yolks

For seafood: Heat broiler.

Divide seafood evenly among 4 individual ramekins or scallop shells. Drizzle 1 tablespoon butter and lemon juice into the ramekins and season with paprika and Old Bay. Set ramekins on baking sheet and place under broiler for about 2 minutes, or until seafood is browned and bubbly. Keep warm.

For sauce: In top half of a double boiler over very low direct heat, melt butter. Add heavy cream to heat but do not boil. Stir in Sauternes, salt, and cayenne pepper. Bring almost to a boil. Place over simmering water in the lower half of the double boiler and stir in yolks. Beat with a whisk until sauce is thickened and smooth.

When ready to serve, cover seafood in each ramekin with sauce and return to broiler until bubbly and starting to brown. Serve immediately. Drizzle remaining sauce over the vegetables you're serving.

Serves 4

EGG DISHES

Chile Egg Puff • Cheese and Corn Pudding • Cheese Soufflé •
Ham-Eggplant-Cheese Soufflé • Spoon Bread

Ham–Eggplant–Cheese Soufflé

Chile Egg Puff

A very close friend of Mrs. Barbara Bush, Louise McClure, wife of Republican Senator James McClure of Idaho, shared this recipe.

> 10 large eggs
> ½ cup all-purpose flour
> 1 teaspoon baking powder
> ½ teaspoon salt
> 8 tablespoons (1 stick) unsalted butter
> 2 cups small curd cottage cheese
> 1 pound Monterey Jack, shredded
> 2 (4-ounce) cans chiles, chopped
> ¼ cup grated Parmesan cheese

Heat oven to 350º. Spray a 9-inch square casserole dish with pan spray.

In the bowl of a stand mixer, slightly beat eggs.

In a separate bowl, sift flour, baking powder, and salt. Add to eggs and beat to combine. With mixer running on low speed, gradually add butter, cottage cheese, and Monterey Jack. Increase speed to medium and continue mixing for 2 minutes. Fold in chiles.

Fill casserole dish and sprinkle top with Parmesan cheese.

Bake for 45 minutes, or until center feels firm to the touch.

Serves 6

Cheese and Corn Pudding

Bobbie and Jack Fitch have been very close friends of the Bush family since 1959. They have been next-door neighbors in Houston since 1993, and in summer they live down the coast from Walker's Point in Maine. This recipe was shared by Mrs. Bobbie Fitch.

4 tablespoons unsalted butter
¼ cup all-purpose flour
2 teaspoons salt
4½ teaspoons sugar
1¾ cups milk
3½ cups fresh corn kernels
3 large eggs
4 scallions, chopped
⅓ cup grated Cheddar cheese

In a saucepan over medium heat, melt butter. Add flour, salt, and sugar and cook, stirring constantly, until bubbly, about 2 minutes. Stir in milk and cook, stirring constantly, until thick. Stir in corn. Remove from heat and let cool to room temperature.

Heat oven to 350º. Butter a 2-quart soufflé dish.

In a bowl, beat eggs until frothy. Fold in corn mixture. Pour into casserole dish and sprinkle top with scallions and Cheddar cheese.

Set casserole in a larger pan and pour in hot water to come 1 inch up the sides. Bake for 45 minutes, until knife inserted 2 inches from rim comes out moist but hot. Pudding will firm up as it cools.

Serves 4

Cheese Soufflé

4 tablespoons unsalted butter
4 tablespoons all-purpose flour
½ teaspoon salt
¼ teaspoon pepper
1 teaspoon dry mustard
½ teaspoon cayenne pepper
3½ cups whole milk
2 cups shredded sharp Cheddar cheese
6 egg yolks, well beaten
6 egg whites
½ teaspoon cream of tartar
Crisp bacon slices, for serving

Heat oven to 350º.

In a saucepan over low heat, melt butter. Stir in flour, salt, pepper, mustard, and cayenne pepper.

Cook, stirring continuously with a whisk, until bubbly, about 3 minutes. Remove from heat and whisk in 2 cups milk. Return to medium heat and bring to a boil, stirring constantly, until thickened to a smooth and velvety texture. Add Cheddar cheese and stir until melted. Remove from heat and stir in egg yolks and 1½ cups milk.

In a separate bowl, beat egg whites and cream of tartar until stiff peaks form. Fold in the hot cheese mixture.

Pour into ungreased 1½-quart soufflé dish or 8 (10-ounce) ramekins. Level top as much as possible and use tip of a teaspoon to make a groove 1 inch from edge and about 1 inch deep. This will give soufflé a high hat look.

Set soufflé dish in larger pan and fill with 1 inch of hot water. Bake for 40–50 minutes, or until puffed and golden brown. Serve immediately with crisp bacon.

Serves 8

Ham-Eggplant-Cheese Soufflé

5 tablespoons unsalted butter
3 cups peeled and diced eggplant
8 ounces ham, chopped
4 tablespoons all-purpose flour
½ teaspoon salt
¼ teaspoon pepper
1 teaspoon dry mustard
½ teaspoon cayenne pepper
3 cups whole milk
1 cup shredded extra sharp Cheddar cheese
6 egg yolks, lightly beaten
6 egg whites
½ teaspoon cream of tartar
Crisp bacon slices, for serving

Heat oven to 350°.

In a heavy-bottomed saucepan over low heat, melt butter. Increase heat to medium and cook eggplant for about 3 minutes, or until partially cooked. Add ham and stir for 1 minute. Remove pan from heat. Using slotted spoon, transfer eggplant-ham mixture to a bowl, draining butter back to saucepan. Set aside.

In the same saucepan over medium heat, add flour, salt, pepper, mustard, and cayenne pepper and cook until bubbly, stirring constantly with a wire whisk. Remove from heat and pour in 2 cups milk while stirring. Return to medium heat and bring to a boil, stirring constantly, until thickened and with a smooth and velvety texture.

Add Cheddar cheese and stir until melted. Remove from heat and stir in egg yolks and 1 cup milk.

In a large bowl, beat egg whites and cream of tartar until stiff. Gently fold half of the egg whites into the hot cheese mixture. Fold in eggplant-ham mixture. Fold in remaining egg whites. Fill 2 ungreased 1½-quart baking dishes to the rim. Level top as much as possible; use tip of a teaspoon to make a groove 1 inch from edge and about 1 inch deep, to give a high hat look. You may also use 10 (10-ounce) ramekins instead.

Set baking dishes in pan of hot water ¾ inch deep. Bake for 40–50 minutes, or until puffed and golden brown. Serve immediately with crisp bacon.

Serves 10

VARIATIONS

Salmon Soufflé: Follow master recipe, substituting 1 cup flaked cooked salmon for the ham and eggplant.

Haddock Soufflé: Follow master recipe, substituting 2 cups flaked cooked haddock for the eggplant and ham and substituting Gruyère for the Cheddar. Increase egg whites to 8 and fold in 1 tablespoon chopped dill.

Mushroom-Cheese Soufflé: Follow master recipe, substituting 2 cups minced mushrooms, well sautéed, for the eggplant and ham.

Yellow Squash-Prosciutto-Cheese Soufflé: Follow master recipe, substituting 2 cups diced yellow squash lightly sautéed with ½ cup sliced shallots for the eggplant and 4 ounces diced prosciutto for the ham.

Ham and Cheese Soufflé: Follow master recipe, without the eggplant. Substitute ½ cup ground boiled ham for the chopped ham.

Tomato-Cheese Soufflé: Follow master recipe, without the eggplant and ham. Substitute tomato juice for the milk.

Spoon Bread

A light and soufflé-like dish.

> 1 cup cornmeal
> 1 teaspoon salt
> 1 teaspoon sugar
> 1 teaspoon baking powder
> ¼ teaspoon baking soda
> 1½ cups boiling water
> 1 tablespoon unsalted butter, melted
> 3 egg yolks
> 1 cup buttermilk
> 3 egg whites

Heat oven to 375°. Grease a 2-quart baking dish.

In a large mixing bowl, combine cornmeal, salt, sugar, baking powder, and baking soda. Carefully pour in boiling water. Stir until lukewarm. Add butter and egg yolks and stir until well blended. Stir in buttermilk.

In a separate bowl, whip egg whites until they form soft peaks. Fold egg whites in batter until well incorporated. Pour into baking dish.

Bake for 45–50 minutes, until knife inserted in center comes out clean. Provide a large serving spoon; this is spoon bread, after all.

Serves 4

VEGETABLES

Stuffed Artichokes • Creamy Asparagus • Asparagus, Tomatoes, Shallots, and Pistachios • Carrot Ring • Corn Pudding • Corn Spoon Bread • Baked Green Beans • Stuffed Mushrooms • Carrot-Stuffed Mushrooms • Nutty Rice Pilaf • Spinach Noodle Ring • Spinach Soufflé • Sweet Potato– Carrot Puree • Walker's Point Yellow Squash Casserole • Baked Squash Casserole • Zucchini Alfredo • Family Baked Zucchini • Baked Stuffed Zucchini • Mixed Vegetable Casserole

Spinach Soufflé

There is one vegetable I cannot use in the kitchens of President (41) and Mrs. Bush. I apologize to all farmers of broccoli and to those who love the vegetable, like me.

I just was not allowed to put broccoli in any meals I prepared ever since he announced, in 1989, to the whole world on national and international television that since he became the President of the United States, his mother could no longer force him to eat broccoli.

Truckloads of broccoli reached the gates of the White House from farmers who sent them in protest of his announcement. The broccoli was distributed. Portions were sent to the White House Residence Kitchen, to the White House Mess, to Camp David. The broccoli was served in many ways: fresh, steamed, boiled, sautéed, baked, fried, breaded, casseroled, scalloped, creamed, cheesed, and—my own favorite—cream of broccoli soup. Even though none of these dishes reached the President's plate, everyone else was gratified. The announcement actually boosted the sale of broccoli all around the nation.

I always have the inclination to sneak in cream of broccoli soup with the President's meal to see if he can detect it. It would be a great story to tell my grandchildren someday that President Bush raved about how great-tasting his "cream of asparagus" soup was and then asked for another helping. I dare not (yet). I really thought it was Brussels sprouts he hated, since I never saw or prepared that vegetable from day one.

Stuffed Artichokes

4 large California artichokes, stems removed
1 cup ripe pitted olives, chopped
½ cup chopped parsley
1 cup chopped seeded tomatoes
1 cup chopped Vidalia onion or other sweet onion
4 teaspoons finely chopped garlic
1 cup bread crumbs
½ cup capers
1 cup shredded Parmesan cheese
2 cups dry white wine

Heat oven to 350°.

With sharp scissors, snip off pointed tips of each artichoke petal.

In a bowl combine olives, parsley, tomatoes, onion, garlic, bread crumbs, capers, and Parmesan cheese. Blend well. Spread each petal as wide as allowed and stuff artichokes.

Transfer to nonreactive Dutch oven. Pour white wine over and around artichokes. Cover and bake for 30–45 minutes, until tender.

Serves 4

Creamy Asparagus

30 asparagus spears
3 tablespoons unsalted butter
3 tablespoons all-purpose flour
½ teaspoon salt
1½ cups heavy cream
⅓ cup split cashews
⅓ cup grated Parmesan cheese
Salt and pepper

Heat oven to 350°. Grease an 11 x 7-inch baking dish.

Snap off tough lower ends of asparagus. Place in a large saucepan with a small amount of water. Cover and cook over medium heat for about 5 minutes or until crisp-tender. Drain. Set aside.

In a saucepan over medium heat, melt butter. Stir in flour and salt and cook until bubbly. Slowly add heavy cream and stir until thick.

Cut asparagus in half crosswise and place half the asparagus in bottom of baking dish. Pour a layer of half the sauce over the asparagus. Sprinkle half the cashews and Parmesan cheese on top of sauce. Season with salt and pepper. Repeat layers. Bake for 30 minutes.

Serves 4–6

Asparagus, Tomatoes, Shallots, and Pistachios

4 tablespoons unsalted butter
2 tablespoons minced shallot
1 tablespoon chopped parsley
1 teaspoon lemon juice

Salt and pepper
1 medium tomato
1 pound fresh asparagus, tough ends snapped
¼ cup chopped pistachios, toasted

In a heavy large skillet over medium heat, melt butter. Add shallot and cook for 2 minutes. Add parsley, lemon juice, and salt and pepper to taste; stir to heat through.

In a small saucepan, boil water. Cut an X in bottom of tomato and place in boiling water for a minute or until tomato skin starts to curl up. Remove tomato from water and peel skin off quickly; cut across in ½-inch-thick slices. Remove and discard seeds and dice tomato evenly. Add tomato cubes to heated shallot mixture. Toss lightly and keep warm.

In another large pot of boiling salted water, cook asparagus for about 2 minutes or until crisp-tender. Drain well. Divide asparagus among 4 plates. Spread shallot-tomato mixture across asparagus spears. Sprinkle with pistachios.

Serves 4

Carrot Ring

Fill the center of the Carrot Ring with buttered peas, sautéed mushrooms, steamed spinach sprinkled with shredded hard-cooked eggs (whites only), baby lima beans, or rice pilaf.

4 cups mashed cooked carrots
4 tablespoons unsalted butter, melted
6 egg yolks
1 cup dry bread crumbs
2 cups milk
½ cup finely chopped onion
2 teaspoons salt
¼ teaspoon pepper
½ teaspoon Worcestershire sauce
6 egg whites, stiffly beaten

Heat oven to 350º. Grease a 12-cup ring mold.

In a bowl, mix carrots, butter, egg yolks, bread crumbs, milk, onion, salt, pepper, and Worcestershire. Fold in egg whites.

Pour into ring mold; set in larger pan and pour in 1 inch hot water. Bake for 45 minutes, or until firm. Invert onto a serving plate and fill center of ring as desired.

Serves 8, or 12 with filling

Corn Pudding

*12 ears white corn or 2 (10-ounce) packages frozen
     white corn, defrosted and drained
1/4 cup all-purpose flour
1 tablespoon sugar
1 teaspoon salt
1/4 teaspoon pepper
3 dashes of cayenne pepper
2 cups light cream
4 tablespoons unsalted butter, melted
3 large eggs, well beaten*

Heat oven to 350º. Grease a 1½-quart baking dish.

Shuck white corn and cut kernels from ears. In a blender, puree half the corn for 4 seconds. In a bowl, combine pureed corn with remaining corn kernels.

Add flour, sugar, salt, pepper, and cayenne pepper. Mix in cream, butter, and eggs, stirring well.

Pour into baking dish. Set dish into a larger pan and pour in 1 inch hot water. Bake, uncovered, for 1 hour and 10 minutes, or until toothpick inserted in center comes out clean.

Serves 6–8

Corn Spoon Bread

1½ cups canned cream-style corn
1 cup yellow cornmeal
¾ cup milk
⅓ cup vegetable oil
3 large eggs, slightly beaten
1 teaspoon salt
1 (4-ounce) jar pickled jalapeño peppers,
    drained and minced
1 cup grated Cheddar cheese

Heat oven to 350°. Butter a baking dish.

In a bowl, mix together corn, cornmeal, milk, vegetable oil, eggs, salt, jalapeños, and cheese.

Pour into baking dish set in a larger pan and pour in 1 inch hot water. Bake for 50–60 minutes, or until a knife comes out clean. Provide guests with a large serving spoon to make the recipe fit its name.

Serves 4–6

Baked Green Beans

This recipe has been a great side dish for all the barbecued entrées I've prepared. I occasionally prepare this recipe in place of regular baked beans. For larger groups entertained at the Bush family residences I simply double the amount of ingredients. One recent event was during the summer of 2004 at the Walker's Point barbecue party to entertain family members and friends (majority were from Texas) of Mandi and George P. Bush, two days before their wedding ceremony. I prepared this dish along with barbecued brisket, spareribs, and chicken and other side dishes for more than two hundred guests. I had Maine volunteers helping serve the food on the buffet lines, and I constantly heard the Texans complimenting the servers on how the food was prepared just as in Texas, and how that made it feel like home. My Mainer friends did not have to reveal to the folks from Texas that the one behind it all was also from Houston, Texas.

12 thick slices smoked bacon, cut into 1-inch pieces
2 garlic cloves, minced
1 large onion, chopped
1 (24-ounce) bottle ketchup
1 (8-ounce) jar Dijon-style mustard
1 cup light brown sugar, packed
Salt and pepper
12 (14.5-ounce) cans cut green beans,
  drained (see Note)

Heat oven to 250°.

In a skillet over medium heat, cook bacon, garlic, and onion until bacon is halfway done and tender. Remove with slotted spoon to a bowl and set aside.

In a large bowl, mix ketchup, mustard, and brown sugar with salt and pepper; blend until sugar dissolves. Combine ketchup mixture with bacon mixture until well incorporated.

Add green beans and with a rubber spatula or wooden spoon, gently fold mixture together.

Transfer mixture into a 13 x 9-inch casserole dish. Bake, covered, for 3 hours.

Serves 12–16

Note: Only canned cut beans work well in this recipe. Do not substitute another form—fresh, frozen, or French-cut.

Another recent event was to entertain more than forty guests during the World Tennis Cup 2004 competition held in Houston. Players, coaches, and guests were scheduled to arrive for lunch at the Bush residence during the second day of the week's event. Unfortunately, the first day of the matches got rained out and affected the next day's schedule. A large number of tennis players could no longer attend the luncheon. Less than three hours before serving time, regrets were sent out to President Bush at the office, and he called the house to announce the bad news to Mrs. Bush. "Cancel the barbecue," Mrs. Bush regretfully passed on to me. She knew I had been barbecuing away and creating a ruckus down in the kitchen since 3:00 A.M., when Sadie, the English spaniel, came down to investigate the first signs of commotion. After some tail wagging and sniffing around, she must have gone upstairs, jumped back in the couple's bed, and woke everyone up.

I was kind of disappointed, too, not because of the time spent preparing the food (barbecued food keeps well in the freezer), but because I missed the chance to meet and feed all the famous players of the World Tennis Cup 2004. I had been honored to serve and feed the previous year's competitors and champions at the Bush residence.

Mr. Bush decided that since they couldn't come to eat with us, we should bring the food to them. It was arranged quickly, and all the effort was not wasted after all. The game coordinators arrived, and at 11:30 that morning, their van left the house loaded with hot food for everyone involved to enjoy at the game sites, hosted by President and Mrs. Bush. I hope I will get my chance to meet and feed another year's tennis champions at the Bush residence.

Stuffed Mushrooms

12 large mushrooms (all the same size), wiped clean
2 tablespoons light olive oil
1 garlic clove, minced
6 scallions, chopped
2 tablespoons chopped parsley
Salt and pepper
4 tablespoons grated Parmesan cheese
1 cup seasoned bread crumbs
4 tablespoons olive oil

Heat oven to 350°. Spray a baking dish large enough to hold mushrooms with pan spray.

Remove stems from mushrooms. Set caps aside. Chop stems finely.

In a saucepan over medium heat, heat light olive oil. Add stems and cook until tender. Add garlic, scallions, and parsley and blend well; season with salt and pepper.

Remove from heat and stir in Parmesan cheese. Toss in bread crumbs lightly, then drizzle olive oil over stuffing, mixing until oil has been completely absorbed.

Fill mushroom caps with stuffing. Place stuffed mushrooms in baking pan and bake for 20 minutes, or until stuffing turns golden brown. Serve hot.

Serves 4–6

Carrot-Stuffed Mushrooms

8 large mushrooms (all the same size), wiped clean
6 tablespoons unsalted butter
1 tablespoon lemon juice
6 medium carrots, peeled and quartered
½ teaspoon sugar

Salt and pepper
2 tablespoons heavy cream

Heat oven to 350°. Remove mushroom stems and reserve for another use.

In a small skillet over medium heat, melt 4 tablespoons butter. Stir in lemon juice and add mushroom caps. Increase heat to medium-high and cook mushrooms until just tender, about 90 seconds on each side. Remove from heat and let mushroom caps cool.

Place carrots in a large saucepan and cover with cold water. Bring to a boil over high heat, then reduce heat and simmer for about 8 minutes, until crisp-tender. Drain.

Place carrots in food processor with remaining 2 tablespoons butter, sugar, and salt and pepper to taste. Pulse to a puree. Add heavy cream and pulse to a smooth puree.

Transfer carrots to pastry bag fitted with a star tip and pipe into mushroom caps. Place on baking sheet and bake for 10 minutes, until hot. You can also place stuffed mushrooms under the broiler and broil until stuffing browns.

Serves 8

Nutty Rice Pilaf

Serve this as a simple side dish or as a ring (see Note)—filled with Creamed Chicken (page 102), colorful steamed vegetables, or a beef or seafood dish—or mound it in the center of a Spinach Soufflé (page 190).

4 cups chicken broth or 4 cups water diluted with 4 chicken bouillon cubes
2 cups long-grain white rice
4 tablespoons unsalted butter
$\frac{1}{2}$ teaspoon finely minced garlic
$\frac{1}{2}$ cup chopped onion
$\frac{1}{4}$ cup chopped carrots
$\frac{1}{4}$ cup baby peas
1 tablespoon dried parsley
$\frac{3}{4}$ cup pine nuts, toasted
1 teaspoon salt

In a large heavy-bottomed saucepan over medium-high heat, bring broth and rice, covered, to a rolling boil. This will take about 10 minutes.

Immediately turn heat down to the lowest setting and continue cooking until rice has absorbed all the broth and is completely cooked, another 15 minutes. Remove lid and fluff cooked rice with fork. Remove pan from heat and set aside, covered.

In a medium skillet over medium heat, melt butter. Add garlic, onion, carrots, and peas and cook until vegetables are tender. Stir in parsley, ½ cup pine nuts, and salt.

Immediately pour sautéed vegetables into pan with fluffed rice and toss to blend well.

Serve as a side dish and top with toasted ¼ cup pine nuts.

Serves 6

Note: For an elegant presentation, spray a 12-inch ring mold lightly with pan spray and line the mold neatly with parchment. Scatter ¼ cup pine nuts in the mold and spoon in the pilaf. Pack the pilaf firmly with your hand, then use a spatula to even it off with the top of the mold. Place a serving dish upside down over the mold and quickly invert. Tap bottom of mold to release the pilaf, then carefully lift off mold. Peel off parchment.

 To line a ring mold with parchment, use the ring mold as a pattern. Draw a circle on parchment paper with a pencil. Cut around circle with a scissors, cutting away pencil marks. Fold parchment circle in half and twice again, creating a cone shape. Align tip of cone with the center of the ring mold and cut away protruding tip. You now have a folded parchment ring. While still folded, snip a few cuts, on both top and bottom open-arched edges toward the center about 1 inch deep. Open folds and press parchment ring on bottom of ring mold coated with pan spray. Snipped edges will overlap each other and rise up to cover the sides partially, yet you will have a complete fitted ring in the bottom of the mold.

Spinach Noodle Ring

This is for our vegetarian guests. We serve this with Zucchini Alfredo (page 193) to make an entrée.

>8 ounces spinach noodles
>2 (10-ounce) packages frozen chopped spinach, defrosted
>8 tablespoons (1 stick) unsalted butter
>1 onion, chopped
>1 cup sour cream
>1 teaspoon salt
>¼ teaspoon black pepper

Heat oven to 350°. Spray an 8-cup ring mold or a 12-inch ring mold well with pan spray.

Cook spinach noodles according to package directions. Drain cooked noodles and set aside in a large bowl. Squeeze chopped spinach to remove all excess moisture and combine with spinach noodles.

In a small skillet over medium heat, melt butter. Add onion and cook until tender. Add to noodle mixture.

In a small bowl, fold sour cream, salt, and pepper together. Add to noodle mixture. Mix well and pour into ring mold. Place in a larger pan and pour in 1 inch hot water.

Bake 45 minutes. Remove from oven and let sit for 10 minutes before running spatula around outside and inside edges of mold. Invert mold onto serving plate. Fill center if desired.

Serves 8

Spinach Soufflé

Fill the center of this soufflé with rice pilaf, plain rice, buttered noodles, corn, or steamed baby carrots.

8 tablespoons unsalted butter
4 tablespoons all-purpose flour
½ teaspoon salt
¼ teaspoon pepper
1 teaspoon dry mustard
½ teaspoon cayenne pepper
2 cups whole milk
6 egg yolks, well beaten
3 (10-ounce) packages frozen chopped spinach, defrosted
½ cup finely chopped onion
½ cup seasoned bread crumbs
6 egg whites

Heat oven to 350º. Spray a 12-inch ring mold with pan spray and dust with flour.

In a heavy-bottomed saucepan over low heat, melt 4 tablespoons butter. Add flour and cook, stirring, until bubbling, about 1 minute. Remove from heat and blend in salt, pepper, mustard, cayenne pepper, and milk.

Return pan to heat and cook, stirring often, until thickened. Add beaten egg yolks, whisking constantly for 3 minutes, or until sauce has thickened and turns velvety in texture. Remove from heat and set aside.

In a medium saucepan over medium heat, combine 4 tablespoons butter and spinach. Bring spinach to a boil in its own liquid; stir constantly until liquid has completely evaporated. Add onion and cook until softened. Add bread crumbs and stir to blend. Stir spinach mixture into sauce. Allow mixture to cool completely.

In a separate bowl, beat egg whites until soft peaks form. Fold into the spinach mixture. Pour into ring mold. Set ring mold in pan of hot water 1 inch deep. Bake for 50–60 minutes, or until firm and tiny bubbles appear between edges of spinach and ring mold. Allow to cool slightly, then invert onto a serving dish.

Serves 12

Sweet Potato–Carrot Puree

This recipe is easy and wonderful to make ahead. Serve with lamb, pork, or chicken—and a green vegetable to fill the center.

> 4 large sweet potatoes
> 2 pounds carrots, cut into chunks
> 4 tablespoons unsalted butter
> ½ cup light cream
> ½ teaspoon salt
> ¼ teaspoon pepper
> ½ teaspoon curry powder
> 2 large eggs, well beaten

Heat oven to 350º. Spray a 12-inch ring mold with pan spray and line it neatly with parchment (see Note, page 188). Spray parchment with pan spray.

Prick sweet potatoes all over with fork, place on aluminum foil, and bake for about 1 hour, until tender. Let cool, and peel. Set aside.

In a saucepan, cover carrots with water. Bring to a boil over high heat, then reduce heat and simmer until carrots are crisp-tender, about 8 minutes. Drain.

In a food processor, combine sweet potatoes, carrots, butter, and cream. Add salt, pepper, and curry powder and pulse to a puree, scraping down sides as necessary. Add eggs and pulse a few times to combine.

Fill mold with puree. You can bake mold now or refrigerate for later baking.

Reduce oven to 325º and bring mold to room temperature.

Bake for 35 minutes, or until a knife inserted 1 inch from edge comes out clean. Allow to cool slightly, then invert onto serving plate. Fill center if desired.

Serves 10–12

Walker's Point Yellow Squash Casserole

Squash became the topic of conversation at the dinner table one night and John Bush, younger brother of the 41st President, claimed he had never liked and had not eaten squash as far as he could remember. Everyone else started giggling because he was, at the same time, devouring some.

> 5 pounds yellow squash, cut into 1-inch rings
> 1 large onion, thinly sliced
> Salt and pepper
> 3 tablespoons unsalted butter
> 3 tablespoons all-purpose flour
> 1 cup milk
> 1 bay leaf
> 1 cup grated Cheddar cheese
> ½ cup bread crumbs

Heat oven to 350°.

In a large saucepan, cover squash and onion with water and boil until tender. Drain well, season with salt and pepper, and set aside.

In a heavy-bottomed saucepan over medium heat, melt butter. Add flour and cook, constantly stirring, until bubbly. Gradually add milk and bay leaf and cook, stirring, until thickened. Stir in cheese until melted. Remove and discard bay leaf.

Gently fold in drained squash. Transfer to a 13 x 9-inch baking dish; top with bread crumbs. Bake for 45 minutes, or until bubbly. Serve hot.

Serves 10–12

Baked Squash Casserole

> 10 medium yellow squash, sliced
> 5 tablespoons unsalted butter

1 yellow onion, chopped
6 large eggs, lightly beaten
1 tablespoon sugar
½ teaspoon salt
½ teaspoon pepper
40 saltine crackers, crushed

Heat oven to 350º. Spray a 13 x 9-inch baking dish with pan spray.

In a large saucepan with a small amount of boiling water, cook squash, covered, until crisp-tender. Drain well. Set aside in a bowl.

In a skillet over medium heat, melt 2 tablespoons butter. Add onion and cook until translucent. Add to squash. Stir in eggs, sugar, salt, and pepper and mix well.

Pour squash mixture into baking dish. Level top. Layer top with cracker crumbs. Press down to level. Melt remaining 3 tablespoons butter and drizzle butter over crackers. Bake for 30–35 minutes. Serve hot.

Serves 8–10

Zucchini Alfredo

2½ pounds zucchini
Salt
8 tablespoons (1 stick) butter, melted
½ cup heavy cream, barely warmed
Freshly ground pepper
Freshly grated nutmeg
1¼ cups freshly grated Parmesan cheese

Cut zucchini lengthwise into ⅛-inch slices. Cut each slice into long spaghettilike strands, about ⅛ inch wide. Or shred zucchini on mandoline fitted with matchstick blade.

Bring 8–10 cups water to boil in a large kettle and add salt. Add zucchini slowly to water so water continues to boil. Cook for about 2 minutes or until crisp-tender. Drain well in colander. Transfer to a serving bowl and toss immediately but gently with butter.

Mix cream, pepper, and nutmeg together in a bowl. Add to hot zucchini. Toss lightly. Add Parmesan cheese and toss gently to coat. Serve immediately.

Serves 8

Family Baked Zucchini

I use baby zucchini for this recipe if available. Cutting diagonally into halves crosswise will yield just the right bite-sized portions.

> 2 tablespoons unsalted butter
> 2 garlic cloves, finely minced
> 1 cup chopped shallots
> 1½ pounds baby zucchini, cut into halves
> 1½ pounds baby pattypan squash, cut into halves
> 1 teaspoon dry mustard
> ½ teaspoon cayenne pepper
> 1 tablespoon curry powder
> Salt and pepper
> 10 large eggs
> 2 cups half-and-half
> 1 cup grated Parmesan cheese

Heat oven to 350º. Grease a 13 x 9-inch baking dish.

In a large saucepan over medium-high heat, melt butter. Add garlic and shallots and cook until shallots are translucent. Add zucchini, squash, mustard, cayenne pepper, curry powder, and salt and pepper to taste. Cook until squash is tender. Remove from heat and keep warm.

In a large bowl, beat eggs. Add half-and-half and beat to combine.

Pour half the egg batter into baking dish. Spread vegetables evenly over eggs, then cover with remaining egg batter. Sprinkle with Parmesan cheese. Bake for 15 minutes, or until center of casserole is firm to the touch.

Serves 12

Baked Stuffed Zucchini

*8 small zucchini (all the same size),
    cut into halves lengthwise
¼ cup light olive oil
1 small onion, finely chopped
4 sprigs parsley, chopped
¼ teaspoon dried thyme
Dash of garlic powder
Pepper
½ cup seasoned dry bread crumbs
⅓ cup grated Parmesan cheese
2 large eggs, well beaten
Butter, as needed*

Heat oven to 350°. Spray a baking sheet with pan spray.

In a medium saucepan over high heat, bring salted water to a rolling boil. Quickly blanch zucchini halves for about 45 seconds. Drain and pat zucchini dry with paper towels. Gently scoop out centers of zucchini, being careful not to tear outside shell; chop and reserve pulp. Arrange zucchini shells on baking sheet and sprinkle with salt. Set aside.

In a saucepan over medium-high heat, heat olive oil. Add onion and cook until translucent. Add chopped zucchini pulp, parsley, thyme, garlic powder, and pepper. Add bread crumbs and stir to blend well. Remove from heat and allow mixture to cool. Stir in Parmesan cheese and beaten eggs. If stuffing is very moist, add additional bread crumbs or cheese.

Mound stuffing in zucchini shells, keeping edges of shells free from stuffing. (This will keep mixture from expanding over edges during baking.) Dot tops with thin slices of butter and bake for 25–30 minutes, until stuffing is firm to the touch.

Serves 8

Mixed Vegetable Casserole

1 (10-ounce) package frozen peas
1 (10-ounce) package frozen baby lima beans
1 (10-ounce) package frozen French-cut green beans
3 green bell peppers, seeded and cut into small strips
1½ cups heavy cream
1½ cups mayonnaise
Salt and pepper
¾ cup grated Parmesan cheese

Heat oven to 325°. Butter a 3-quart casserole dish.

Bring a large pot of salted water to a boil. Add peas, lima beans, and green beans and boil just enough for frozen vegetables to separate with a fork. Drain and allow vegetables to cool. Add bell peppers.

In a large mixing bowl, mix heavy cream and mayonnaise together. Add vegetables and gently fold together. Season with salt and pepper.

Spoon into casserole dish. Sprinkle top with Parmesan cheese.

Bake for 50 minutes, or until golden brown and puffy on top.

Serves 8

SAUCES FOR ALL OCCASIONS

Aïoli • Béarnaise Sauce • Cheese Sauce • Hollandaise Sauce • Rich Mornay Sauce • Polonaise Sauce • Velouté Sauce • White Sauce • Almond Velvet Sauce • Elizabeth's Barbecue Sauce • Creamy Curry Sauce • Piquant Sauce • Raisin Sauce • Satay Sauce • Sweet-and-Sour Sauce • Sweet and Spicy Sauce • Pesto • Tomato-Mushroom Sauce • Tomato-Prosciutto Sauce • Walker's Point Butterscotch Sauce • Mrs. Howe's Chocolate Sauce • Quick Chocolate Sauce • Coffee and Rum Sauce • English Custard Sauce • Sabayon Sauce

Elizabeth's Barbecue Sauce

Aïoli

Serve with crudités or cold cuts. Also great as an egg roll dip.

>6 garlic cloves, minced or pressed
>Salt
>2 egg yolks
>½ cup olive oil
>2 teaspoons lemon juice or tarragon vinegar
>Pepper

In a medium bowl, combine garlic, salt, and 1 egg yolk. Whisk until well blended. Add the remaining yolk and whisk until light.

Slowly drip in olive oil, whisking constantly until sauce begins to thicken. Whisk in lemon juice. Continue to add oil, gradually increasing to a steady trickle. Enough oil has been added when sauce becomes really thick. Season with pepper to taste.

Makes 1 cup

Béarnaise Sauce

Serve warm, with roast beef, steaks, lamb, chicken, or fish.

>3 medium shallots, chopped
>¼ teaspoon dried chervil
>2 teaspoons finely chopped tarragon
>4 black peppercorns, crushed
>2 tablespoons white wine vinegar
>3 egg yolks
>12 tablespoons (1½ sticks) unsalted butter, cut into pieces
>Salt and cayenne pepper
>½ teaspoon each chopped tarragon and parsley, for serving

In a medium saucepan over medium heat, combine shallots, chervil, tarragon, peppercorns, and vinegar; cook until liquid is reduced by half.

In the top half of a double boiler over barely simmering water, whisk egg yolks. Do not allow water to boil or touch bottom of top half of double boiler. Strain vinegar through a fine sieve into the egg yolks; whisk until blended. Discard solids.

Whisking constantly, add butter piece by piece, making sure each piece is melted and absorbed before adding the next piece. The sauce should be smooth like mayonnaise. Adjust seasoning with salt and cayenne pepper. Stir in chopped tarragon and fresh parsley.

Makes about 2 cups

Cheese Sauce

Serve hot over lightly cooked vegetables or over broiled chicken or fish.

> 2 tablespoons unsalted butter
> 2 tablespoons all-purpose flour
> 1 cup milk
> ½ teaspoon Dijon style mustard
> 1 teaspoon chicken bouillon cube, crumbled
> 4 drops Tabasco sauce
> ¼ cup dry sherry
> ¾ cup grated Cheddar cheese

In a saucepan over medium heat, melt butter. Stir in flour, stirring constantly until bubbly. Gradually add milk and whisk until creamy and thickened. Add mustard, bouillon cube, Tabasco, and sherry. Add cheese and stir until melted through.

Makes 2 cups

Hollandaise Sauce

I serve this over steamed vegetables and broiled fish.

> 3 egg yolks
> 4 tablespoons simmering water
> 1½ tablespoons lemon juice
> 8 tablespoons (1 stick) unsalted butter, melted and kept warm
> Salt
> Dash of paprika

In a double boiler or glass bowl set over a saucepan of simmering water, whisk egg yolks constantly for about 1 minute, until light. Add simmering water, 1 tablespoon at a time, whisking constantly between additions until mixture thickens, 1–2 minutes. Gradually stir in lemon juice. Remove double boiler from heat. Slowly whisk in melted butter. Add salt and serve warm, garnished with paprika.

Makes 1¼ cups

Rich Mornay Sauce

> 4 tablespoons unsalted butter
> 4 tablespoons all-purpose flour
> 3 cups chicken broth
> 1 teaspoon salt
> ¼ teaspoon white pepper
> ¼ teaspoon grated nutmeg
> ½ teaspoon paprika
> 4 egg yolks
> ¾ cup heavy cream
> ¼ cup grated Parmesan or shredded Swiss cheese

In a saucepan over low heat, melt butter. Stir in flour and cook, stirring until well blended and bubbly. Gradually stir in broth. Increase heat to medium-high and bring to a boil, stirring constantly. Boil for 1 minute, or until sauce thickens. Season with salt, pepper, nutmeg, and paprika. Remove from heat.

In a bowl, whisk together egg yolks and heavy cream. Pour half of the sauce into the bowl, whisking, to temper the eggs. Return this to the saucepan and stir well. Return the saucepan to medium-low heat and cook, stirring, until heated through. Add cheese gradually, stirring until cheese melts.

Makes about 3 cups

Polonaise Sauce

Serve hot with freshly steamed carrots, green beans, or cauliflower.

> 1½ tablespoons unsalted butter
> 1 tablespoon all-purpose flour
> ¼ teaspoon salt
> 1 cup chicken broth
> 2 egg yolks, lightly beaten
> 1 tablespoon lemon juice
> Dash of paprika

In a saucepan over medium-high heat, melt butter. Add flour and salt; stir and cook until bubbly. Stir in chicken broth and bring mixture to a boil, stirring constantly until sauce thickens.

In a bowl, whisk egg yolks until light.

Blend half of thickened stock into egg yolks. Scrape egg mixture back into saucepan and cook over low heat, stirring constantly, for 1 minute. Stir in lemon juice and paprika.

Makes 1 cup

Velouté Sauce

Serve to complement broiled meat, chicken, or fish.

> 2 tablespoons unsalted butter
> 2 tablespoons all-purpose flour
> 1 cup chicken, veal, or fish broth
> Salt
> Dash of white pepper
> 1/8 teaspoon grated nutmeg

In a saucepan over low heat, melt butter. Stir in flour and cook until bubbly. Gradually stir in broth. Bring to a boil, stirring constantly. Boil for 1 minute. Season with salt, white pepper, and nutmeg.

Makes 1 cup

White Sauce

Perfect for creamed and scalloped dishes. For a thinner sauce, decrease butter and flour to 1 tablespoon each.

> 2 tablespoons unsalted butter
> 2 tablespoons all-purpose flour
> 1/4 teaspoon salt
> 1/8 teaspoon pepper
> 1 cup milk

In a saucepan over low heat, melt butter. Stir in flour, salt, and pepper and cook until bubbly. Stir in milk. Bring to a boil, stirring constantly, until thickened, smooth, and velvety.

Makes 1 cup

Almond Velvet Sauce

Great with chicken, turkey, Cornish game hen, or quail.

>   2 tablespoons unsalted butter
>   2 tablespoons all-purpose flour
>   1 cup chicken broth
>   Salt
>   Dash of white pepper
> $\frac{1}{8}$ teaspoon grated nutmeg
> $\frac{1}{4}$ cup blanched slivered almonds, toasted

In a saucepan over low heat, melt butter. Stir in flour and cook until bubbly. Stir in broth. Bring to a boil, stirring constantly. Boil for 1 minute. Blend in salt, white pepper, and nutmeg. Stir in almonds just before serving.

Makes about 1 cup

Elizabeth's Barbecue Sauce

My dear wife, Elizabeth, claims she can outcook me anytime of the day. I do not disagree with her. Most of the time I savor someone else's toil. After being on my feet cooking all day at work, I would rather sit and watch television when I get home and just wait for my wife to call out, "Time to eat!"

Use as a marinade or brush on during broiling and grilling your favorite cut of meat. This sauce may be boiled and served hot as a dipping sauce for egg rolls.

1 (14-ounce) bottle ketchup
1 (12-ounce) bottle chili sauce
1 (8-ounce) jar Dijon-style mustard
1½ cups red wine
½ cup vegetable oil
½ cup soy sauce
1 tablespoon Tabasco sauce
½ cup lemon juice
4 tablespoons Worcestershire sauce
2 tablespoons liquid smoke
1 cup brown sugar, packed
1 tablespoon cracked black pepper
1 teaspoon ground cloves
8 garlic cloves, chopped

In a 2-quart glass or plastic container, combine ketchup, chili sauce, mustard, wine, oil, soy sauce, Tabasco, lemon juice, Worcestershire, liquid smoke, brown sugar, pepper, cloves, and garlic. Shake well. Keep covered and refrigerated.

Makes about 9 cups

Creamy Curry Sauce

Serve hot over hard-cooked eggs, broiled chicken, or quail. This sauce may be used as the base for Shrimp Curry (page 164) or Chicken Curry (page 113).

4 tablespoons unsalted butter
2 onions, finely chopped
1 garlic clove
$\frac{1}{2}$ teaspoon grated fresh ginger
4 tablespoons all-purpose flour
$\frac{1}{2}$ teaspoon salt
$\frac{1}{4}$ teaspoon white pepper
2 cups milk
1 tablespoon curry powder

In a medium saucepan over low heat, melt butter. Add onions, garlic, and ginger and cook for 2 minutes. Remove garlic and discard; only a hint of its flavor is needed. Blend in flour, salt, and pepper and let bubble for 1 minute. Gradually stir in milk.

Bring to boil, stirring constantly until thickened, smooth, and velvety. Stir in curry powder and mix well.

Makes about 2 cups

Piquant Sauce

Serve hot with roast pork or use for reheating leftover meats.

4 tablespoons unsalted butter
1 large onion, diced
3 tablespoons all-purpose flour
1 cup white wine vinegar
1 cup dry white wine
Salt and pepper
2 dill pickles, finely chopped
1 teaspoon chopped tarragon
2 teaspoons chopped parsley
$\frac{1}{4}$ teaspoon dried chervil
1 beef bouillon cube, crumbled
$\frac{1}{4}$ cup hot water

In a saucepan over low heat, melt butter. Add onion and cook until translucent. Sprinkle in flour and cook, stirring, 10 minutes, until browned.

Mix together white wine vinegar and dry white wine. Add to saucepan. Whisk until smooth and creamy. Season with salt and pepper and simmer for 15 minutes. Add pickles, tarragon, parsley, and chervil. Dissolve bouillon in water and add to sauce. Simmer for 10 minutes.

Makes 3 cups

Raisin Sauce

Serve hot with grilled ham steaks or boiled ham.

> 1/4 cup all-purpose flour
> 1 1/2 tablespoons light brown sugar
> 1 1/2 tablespoons dry mustard
> Salt and pepper
> 1 1/2 cups boiling water
> 2 tablespoons white wine vinegar
> 1 tablespoon lemon juice
> 1/3 cup chopped golden raisins
> 1/3 cup crushed pineapple, drained
> 2 tablespoons unsalted butter

In a medium saucepan, combine flour, sugar, mustard, and salt and pepper to taste. Stir in boiling water, a little at a time, stirring constantly to produce a smooth sauce. Add white wine vinegar and lemon juice; simmer over medium heat for 7 minutes. Add raisins and pineapple, reduce heat to low, and cook for 3 more minutes.

Just before serving, add butter and stir well.

Makes about 1 3/4 cups

Satay Sauce

Serve hot over skewered grilled cubes of beef or chicken.

> 2 cups boiling water
> ¼ cup shredded unsweetened coconut
> 1 large onion, diced
> 2 garlic cloves, chopped
> 6 small dried red chiles
> 1 tablespoon pine nuts
> 1 tablespoon grated lemon zest
> 2 tablespoons peanut oil
> ¾ cup crunchy peanut butter
> 1 teaspoon sugar
> Salt

In a medium bowl, combine boiling water and coconut and allow coconut to soak 30 minutes, or until water has cooled off.

In a blender or food processor, puree onion, garlic, chiles, pine nuts, and lemon zest. Transfer to a saucepan. Add peanut oil and cook over low heat for 3 minutes.

Strain coconut through fine sieve set over a bowl. Discard coconut pulp. Add coconut milk to saucepan and bring to a boil, stirring constantly. Reduce heat; add crunchy peanut butter, sugar, and salt. Simmer for another 3 minutes.

Makes 2 cups

Sweet-and-Sour Sauce

Great for fried breaded chicken nuggets, fried breaded fish or shrimp, or fried egg rolls.

⅔ cup brown sugar, packed
⅔ cup granulated sugar
1 cup ketchup
½ teaspoon ground cinnamon
6 whole cloves
2 slices fresh ginger
Lemon juice
1 tablespoon cornstarch
1 cup pineapple juice
2 tablespoons pineapple chunks
3 maraschino cherries, chopped
Salt

In a small saucepan, mix sugars, ketchup, cinnamon, cloves, ginger, and lemon juice to taste. Bring to a boil. Lower heat and simmer for 15 minutes, stirring occasionally.

Combine cornstarch and pineapple juice and add to saucepan. Continue simmering, stirring, until thickened. Remove from heat and stir in pineapple chunks and cherries. Adjust taste with lemon juice and salt. Set aside to cool.

Remove and discard cloves and ginger slices.

Makes about 2 cups

Sweet and Spicy Sauce

Great with Baked Breaded Chicken (page 91).

1 cup red currant jelly
1 (6-ounce) can frozen orange juice

4 tablespoons dry sherry
1 teaspoon dry mustard
⅛ teaspoon ground ginger
¼ teaspoon Tabasco sauce

In a small saucepan, combine jelly, orange juice, sherry, mustard, ginger, and Tabasco. Stir. Simmer over medium heat until smooth.

Makes 1½ cups

Pesto

Serve with pasta.

1 cup basil leaves, packed
2 garlic cloves, chopped
½ teaspoon salt
⅓ cup pine nuts
1 cup olive oil
5 tablespoons grated Parmesan cheese

In a blender, combine basil leaves, garlic, salt, pine nuts and chop finely.

With motor running, add olive oil in thin stream. Scrape down sides to make sure all solids are well mixed. Continue to blend until mixture becomes smooth. Add Parmesan cheese during last part of mixing, giving the machine one small burst to blend ingredients well.

Transfer to a small skillet and simmer before serving with pasta. Leftover sauce may be refrigerated in a sealed container for up to 1 month.

Makes about 2 cups

Tomato-Mushroom Sauce

Serve hot with pasta. Also delicious when served with an omelet, leftover chicken, or leftover turkey.

> 1 slice bacon, diced
> 1 tablespoon all-purpose flour
> 1½ teaspoons sugar
> ⅛ teaspoon salt
> 1 cup tomato juice
> 1 tablespoon unsalted butter
> ¼ pound mushrooms, chopped

In a small saucepan over medium heat, cook bacon. Blend in flour, sugar, and salt and cook, stirring, until bubbly. Remove from heat. Stir in tomato juice. Return to heat and bring to a boil; cook 1 minute, stirring constantly.

In a separate saucepan over medium heat, melt butter. Add mushrooms and cook until browned. Combine mushrooms and sauce.

Makes 2 cups

Tomato-Prosciutto Sauce

Bill Busch, a Mainer fishing partner of President Bush, shared this recipe in response to what Bill read in one of Mrs. Bush's books. Mr. Bush loves to do errands and has the habit of picking up stuff that he does not really need. In one of his escapades, he went to a wholesale store and brought home jars of pasta sauce and asked Mrs. Bush to prepare it for their dinner during my weekend breaks. That incident was mentioned in one of her published books. Bill read about how his fishing buddy was being fed with ready-made sauce by his wife, and he immediately sent me this recipe. I tested the recipe and received high acceptability ratings. It is also great when served the day it's made over angel hair, penne, or bow tie pasta.

> 2 tablespoons extra virgin olive oil
> ¾ pound prosciutto, cut into thin strips

2 garlic cloves, minced
1 small onion, chopped
1 (28-ounce) can plum tomatoes
2 tablespoons chopped parsley
2 tablespoons chopped basil
1 tablespoon chopped oregano
¼ teaspoon salt
⅛ teaspoon pepper
½ teaspoon hot pepper flakes
½ teaspoon sugar

In a large pot over low heat, heat olive oil. Add prosciutto, garlic, and onion and cook until onion is translucent. Add plum tomatoes and bring to a boil. Reduce heat; add parsley, basil, oregano, salt, pepper, hot pepper flakes, and sugar and allow sauce to simmer for 40 minutes.

Makes about 3 cups

Walker's Point Butterscotch Sauce

Jebby, the youngest son of Florida Governor John Ellis Bush (Jeb), will not touch his ice cream unless it's topped with this sauce. When the sweet aroma of butterscotch fills the air in the kitchen, it's a clear indication of Jebby's homecoming for his summer visits to Walker's Point.

4 tablespoons unsalted butter
⅔ cup brown sugar, packed
⅓ cup light corn syrup
1 egg yolk
¼ cup water
½ teaspoon vanilla extract

In a heavy saucepan over low heat, melt butter. Add brown sugar and light corn syrup. Cook, stirring constantly, until sugar dissolves. Remove from heat but keep warm.

In a separate bowl, beat egg yolk and water together. Combine egg-water mixture with the sugar-butter mixture and return to low heat. Cook, stirring, until thick and smooth. Stir in vanilla.

Makes 1 cup

Mrs. Howe's Chocolate Sauce

This recipe was shared with Mrs. Barbara Bush when she and Mr. Bush were newlyweds. Bill Howe and 41st President George Bush were great friends in high school, and Bill's parents lived in New Haven, Connecticut. Mr. and Mrs. Howe were very nice to the young couple, and their son, Bill, became George W. Bush's godfather.

We always keep a jar of this sauce in the refrigerator. It's still the best.

2 ounces unsweetened chocolate
2 tablespoons unsalted butter
$\frac{2}{3}$ cup boiling water
4 tablespoons light corn syrup
2 cups sugar
1 teaspoon vanilla extract
Salt

In top half of a double boiler over simmering water, melt chocolate. Add butter and blend thoroughly. Pour in boiling water slowly while stirring constantly. Add corn syrup and sugar and stir until well mixed and dissolved. Bring to a boil, remove from heat, and allow mixture to cool. Add vanilla and salt. Serve hot.

Makes 1½ cups

Quick Chocolate Sauce

Perfect for sundaes.

> ½ *cup semisweet chocolate chips*
> ½ *cup heavy cream*

In a small saucepan over low heat, melt chocolate gently. Pour in heavy cream and stir to combine. Remove from heat.

Makes 1 cup

Coffee and Rum Sauce

Great for fresh fruit salads.

> ½ *cup hot strong black coffee*
> *2 teaspoons sugar*
> *2 egg yolks*
> *1 teaspoon cornstarch*
> *1 tablespoon whole milk*
> *2 tablespoons dark rum*

In top half of double boiler, combine coffee and sugar. Remove from heat and cool slightly. Add egg yolks, one at a time, combining well after each addition.

In the bottom half of double boiler, bring water just below simmering point. Return top of double boiler to simmering water and cook coffee-egg mixture for 2 minutes.

In a measuring cup, mix cornstarch and milk together and add to hot coffee-egg mixture. Stir constantly until sauce thickens. Stir in rum and serve hot.

Makes about 1 cup

English Custard Sauce

⅓ cup sugar
1 tablespoon cornstarch
2 cups milk
2 tablespoons unsalted butter
6 egg yolks
1½ teaspoons vanilla extract
½ cup heavy cream

In a medium saucepan, combine sugar and cornstarch. Gradually add milk, stirring until smooth. Add butter and cook over medium heat, stirring, until thickened and at a boil. Boil for about 1 minute. Remove from heat.

In another bowl, beat yolks slightly. Add a little hot mixture into the egg yolks and beat well. Stir egg mixture back into saucepan and cook over medium heat, stirring constantly just until the sauce boils. Remove from heat again and stir in vanilla. Strain through a fine sieve immediately into a bowl.

Refrigerate until cooled. Stir in heavy cream. Refrigerate until ready to serve.

Makes 2½ cups

Sabayon Sauce

*On my trip to Malta during the summit meeting between Russian President Mikhail Gorb...
President Bush in 1989, the U.S. delegation was to host dinner onboard the USS Belknap, ...
the Russian delegations. Executive Pastry Chef Roland Mesnier of the White House asked n...
the Raspberry Parfait he prepared for the occasion and for me to prepare the Sabayon Sau...
his version of the sauce. He sent me off with a very simple and practical hint. He told me t...
palm underneath the bottom of the bowl as I pour the hot sugar syrup while whipping the ...
The bowl bottom will turn warm to the touch. Continue whipping and stop only when the ...
tom feels cool to the touch. "You'll never go wrong," he said. I accomplished the task for hin...
master skills worked well for me across the Atlantic Ocean.*

⅓ cup water
½ cup sugar
½ tablespoon white corn syrup
3 egg yolks, at room temperature
1 cup heavy cream
¼ cup clear raspberry brandy (eau de vie)

In a small saucepan, boil water, sugar, and corn syrup together. Set sugar syrup a...
keep hot.

In a mixing bowl, beat yolks at medium speed until pale yellow. Turn mixer...
speed. In a steady stream pour hot sugar syrup into egg yolks without touchi...
whisk. Reduce speed to medium and continue beating until mixture thickens a...
sugar mixture turns almost cool.

In another mixing bowl, beat heavy cream to soft peaks. Fold egg-sugar...
gently into whipped cream. Fold in brandy. Cover and refrigerate before servi...

Makes about 2 cups

MUFFINS, QUICK BREADS, BISCUITS, AND DINNER ROLLS

Walker's Point Blueberry Muffins • Blueberry Crumb Muffins • Walker's Point Blueberry Cornmeal Muffins • Walker's Point Strawberry Muffins • Walker's Point Banana Muffins • Sour Cream Bundt Coffee Cake • Banana Bread • Zucchini Bread • Buttermilk Biscuits • Sour Cream Biscuits • White House Cheese Blisters • White House Crackers • Generations Cheese-Stuffed Bread • Puffed Cheese Rolls • Favorite Butterhorns • Homemade Philippine Rolls • Chamorro Dinner Rolls

Assorted Muffins: Blueberry, Strawberry, Banana

Walker's Point Blueberry Muffins

2 cups all-purpose flour
1 teaspoon baking soda
½ teaspoon salt
½ teaspoon ground cinnamon
⅛ teaspoon grated nutmeg
8 tablespoons (1 stick) unsalted butter
½ cup granulated sugar
½ cup light brown sugar, packed
½ cup orange juice
2 large eggs, lightly beaten
1 teaspoon vanilla extract
1 cup blueberries
1½ tablespoons grated orange zest

Set oven rack in center of oven. Heat oven to 350°. Coat 12 muffin cups with pan spray.

In a bowl, sift flour, baking soda, salt, cinnamon, and nutmeg twice. Set aside.

In a medium saucepan over medium heat, melt butter. Blend in granulated sugar and brown sugar. Remove from heat, stir in orange juice, eggs, and vanilla. Stir in the flour mixture and gently fold in blueberries and orange zest. Spoon batter into muffin tin, filling cups almost to the top.

Bake until muffins are golden brown and cake tester inserted into 1 or 2 muffins comes out clean, about 25 minutes. Let rest in pan about 5 minutes, and then remove muffins to a rack to cool.

Makes 12 muffins

Blueberry Crumb Muffins

FOR CRUMB TOPPING

⅓ cup all-purpose flour
⅓ cup sugar
¼ teaspoon ground cinnamon
4 tablespoons cold unsalted butter,
        cut into small pieces

FOR MUFFINS

2 cups all-purpose flour
¼ cup sugar
1 tablespoon baking powder
1½ teaspoons grated nutmeg
1 large egg
1 cup milk
3 tablespoons unsalted butter, melted
1 cup blueberries

For crumb topping: In a small bowl, mix flour, sugar, and cinnamon together. Cut in butter until mixture resembles coarse crumbs. Chill until ready to use.

For muffins: Heat oven to 400º. Spray muffin tin (2 ½-inch) with pan spray or line with paper liners.

In a large bowl, sift together flour, sugar, baking powder, and nutmeg.

In a medium bowl, beat egg, milk, and butter until well blended. Add egg mixture to flour mixture, stirring just until dry ingredients are moistened. Gently stir in blueberries with last few strokes.

Fill muffin tin about three-quarters full. Sprinkle tops evenly with crumb topping. Bake for 25–30 minutes, or until well browned. Serve warm.

Makes 12 muffins

Walker's Point Blueberry Cornmeal Muffins

These complement chowder, casseroles, and salad. Leftover muffins may be frozen for up to 1 month. Simply reheat and serve. President Bush's favorite breakfast treat is two partially thawed muffins in halves, each half topped with a pat of butter and broiled until the edges start to turn brown and crisp. Serve with maple or fruit syrup.

> 1 cup yellow cornmeal
> 1 cup all-purpose flour
> 1 tablespoon baking powder
> 1/4 teaspoon salt
> 1/2 cup sugar
> 1 cup milk
> 1 large egg, lightly beaten
> 1/4 cup vegetable shortening, melted
> 1 cup blueberries

Set oven rack in center of oven. Heat oven to 400°. Spray muffin tin with pan spray or line with paper liners.

In a large bowl, combine cornmeal, flour, baking powder, and salt. Set aside.

In a separate bowl, beat sugar, milk, egg, and shortening together. Gradually whisk in dry ingredients until moistened. Fold in blueberries gently until well coated. Fill muffin cups to the rim. Bake for 20 minutes, until cake tester comes out clean.

Makes 12 muffins

Walker's Point Strawberry Muffins

¾ cup shredded unsweetened coconut
2 cups all-purpose flour
1 teaspoon baking soda
½ teaspoon salt
1 cup hulled strawberries
8 tablespoons (1 stick) unsalted butter
½ cup granulated sugar
½ cup light brown sugar, packed
2 eggs, lightly beaten
1 teaspoon vanilla extract

Heat oven to 350°. Spray muffin tins with pan spray or line with paper liners.

Spread coconut on baking sheet and toast until golden, 8–10 minutes. Set aside.

In a large bowl, sift together flour, baking soda, and salt. Set aside.

Mash strawberries with a fork in a bowl. Do not puree, just mash. Set aside.

In a medium saucepan over medium heat, melt butter. Blend in granulated and light brown sugars. Remove from heat and add mashed strawberries, eggs, and vanilla; stir until smooth.

Stir into flour mixture. Fold in all but 2 tablespoons toasted coconut.

Fill muffin tins to the top of each cup. Sprinkle remaining 2 tablespoons coconut over each muffin.

Bake until golden brown and cake tester comes out clean, 25–30 minutes. Let rest in pan for about 5 minutes and then remove muffins to a rack to cool.

Makes 12 muffins

Walker's Point Banana Muffins

2 cups all-purpose flour
1 teaspoon baking soda
½ teaspoon salt
8 tablespoons (1 stick) unsalted butter
½ cup granulated sugar
½ cup light brown sugar, packed
1 cup mashed bananas
2 eggs, lightly beaten
1 teaspoon vanilla extract
½ cup coarsely chopped walnuts
1½ teaspoons grated lemon zest

Heat oven to 350°. Spray muffin tins with pan spray or line with paper liners.

In a large bowl, sift flour, baking soda, and salt together. Set aside.

In a medium saucepan over medium heat, melt butter. Blend in granulated sugar and brown sugar. Remove from heat. Stir in bananas, eggs, and vanilla until smooth.

Stir into the sifted dry ingredients; fold in walnuts and lemon zest. Spoon batter into muffin tin.

Bake until muffins are golden brown and cake tester comes out clean, 25–30 minutes. Let rest in pan for about 5 minutes. Remove muffins to a rack to cool.

Makes 12 muffins

Sour Cream Bundt Coffee Cake

FOR CRUMBS

½ cup light brown sugar, packed
1 teaspoon ground cinnamon
1 tablespoon unsalted butter, melted
1 tablespoon all-purpose flour
½ cup chopped walnuts

FOR BATTER

1½ cups all-purpose flour
1 cup sugar
1 tablespoon baking powder
½ teaspoon baking soda
¼ teaspoon salt
1 cup sour cream (low-fat is okay)
2 large eggs
Confectioners' sugar, for garnish (optional)

Heat oven to 350°. Spray a Bundt pan with pan spray and dust lightly with flour.

For crumbs: In a bowl, mix brown sugar, cinnamon, butter, flour, and walnuts until crumbly. Set aside.

For batter: Sift flour, sugar, baking powder, baking soda, and salt twice. Transfer sifted ingredients to mixing bowl and beat in sour cream and eggs until smooth.

Pour in enough batter to cover bottom of Bundt pan. Sprinkle crumbs over batter. Pour in remaining batter to cover crumbs.

Bake for 20 minutes, or until cake tester comes out clean. Allow to cool slightly. Loosen edges and invert onto a serving plate. Remove pan. Dust with confectioners' sugar, if desired. Cut into wedges and serve warm.

Makes 1 cake

Banana Bread

This banana bread is shared by Ashley Bush, Neil Bush's youngest daughter. Ashley and her father tested this recipe, which came from a friend of Ashley's. The finished product tasted great, even though they discovered during cleanup that the buttermilk had never been opened. Each time Ashley visits Walker's Point, I bake this bread for her in a 12-inch ring mold. Each time, we assure each other, buttermilk has not been used.

8 tablespoons (1 stick) unsalted butter
1¼ cups sugar
2 large eggs
4 ripe bananas, mashed
1 teaspoon vanilla extract
4 tablespoons buttermilk
2 cups all-purpose flour
1½ teaspoons baking soda
1 teaspoon salt
1 cup chopped pecans (optional)

Heat oven to 350°. Butter and flour a 9 x 5-inch loaf pan.

In bowl of a mixer, cream butter and sugar until fluffy. Add eggs, one at a time, beating well after each addition. Add bananas, vanilla, and buttermilk.

In a separate bowl, sift together flour, baking soda, and salt. Gradually add to wet mixture and stir to combine and moisten. Stir in the pecans, if desired.

Pour batter into pan. Bake for 45–50 minutes, or until golden brown. Serve at room temperature.

Makes 1 loaf

Note: This batter is enough for 2 (12-inch) ring molds.

Zucchini Bread

At the Vice President's House, we sometimes described this bread as "Food of the Gods." Doubling the recipe and baking the zucchini bread in miniature loaf pans will yield 12 loaves (reduce baking time by half), perfect for Christmas holiday presents for friends and neighbors.

2 cups all-purpose flour
¾ cup granulated sugar
¾ cup light brown sugar, packed
1 tablespoon baking powder
2 teaspoons baking soda
1 teaspoon salt
1 tablespoon ground cinnamon
3 large eggs
1 cup vegetable oil
1 tablespoon vanilla extract
2 cups grated zucchini
¾ cup golden raisins
½ cup broken walnuts

Heat oven to 325°. Spray a 9 x 5-inch loaf pan with pan spray.

In a large bowl combine flour, sugars, baking powder, baking soda, salt, and cinnamon. Set aside.

In a separate bowl, stir together eggs, oil, vanilla, and zucchini. Add wet ingredients to dry. Mix just to combine and moisten.

Fold raisins and walnuts into batter. Pour into loaf pan. Bake for 50 minutes, until cake tester comes out clean.

Makes 1 loaf

Buttermilk Biscuits

2 cups all-purpose flour
1 tablespoon baking powder
½ teaspoon baking soda
½ teaspoon salt
1 teaspoon sugar
⅓ cup unsalted butter, cold and cut
        into pieces
¾ cup buttermilk

Set oven rack on highest shelf. Heat oven to 400°. Spray a baking sheet with pan spray.

In a bowl, sift together flour, baking powder, baking soda, salt, and sugar. Cut butter into dry ingredients until mixture resembles coarse cornmeal. Add buttermilk and stir to make a dough.

Turn dough onto lightly floured surface and form into ball. Flatten dough with your hands to about ¾ inch thick. Cut out biscuits with a 2-inch biscuit cutter. Place on baking sheet and bake for 10 minutes, until tops are lightly browned.

Makes about 12 biscuits

Sour Cream Biscuits

1½ cups all-purpose flour
½ cup cornmeal
2 teaspoons baking powder
½ teaspoon baking soda
½ teaspoon salt
8 tablespoons (1 stick) unsalted butter,
        cold and cut into pieces
⅓ cup buttermilk

⅓ cup sour cream
1 egg white, beaten

Set oven rack on highest shelf. Heat oven to 425°. Spray a baking sheet with pan spray.

In a bowl, sift together flour, cornmeal, baking powder, baking soda, and salt. Cut butter into dry ingredients until mixture resembles coarse cornmeal. Add buttermilk and sour cream and stir to make a dough.

Turn dough onto lightly floured surface and form into ball. Flatten dough with your hands to about 1 inch thick. Cut out biscuits with a cutter. Place on baking sheet, brush tops with egg white, and bake for 15–20 minutes, until tops are lightly browned.

Makes about 12 biscuits

White House Cheese Blisters

This was a recipe shared by the White House Mess Stewards to the Stewards at the Vice President's House. These cracker-like "blisters" are cut into assorted shapes before baking. You may make these blisters by rolling the dough ½ inch thick and cutting into 4-inch sticks. Twist sticks as you transfer them to baking sheets if you like.

1 cup all-purpose flour
½ teaspoon salt
¼ teaspoon cayenne pepper
8 tablespoons (1 stick) unsalted
*   butter, at room temperature*
1 cup grated Cheddar cheese
3 tablespoons ice water

Heat oven to 425°.

In a bowl, sift together flour, salt, and cayenne pepper. Cut in butter and cheese until mixture resembles coarse cornmeal.

White House Cheese Blisters

Add water 1 tablespoon at a time, mixing well with a fork after each addition, until mixture forms a soft dough. Form dough into a ball, wrap with plastic, and chill for 30 minutes, until firm and easy to handle.

On a floured work surface, roll dough. Cut into strips (see headnote). Brush off excess flour. Transfer strips to baking sheets and bake for about 10 minutes, until golden brown. Biscuits will puff and blister during baking.

Makes 6–8 dozen blisters

White House Crackers

This recipe was also shared by the White House Stewards to the Vice President's Stewards earlier in my career.

> *4 cups all-purpose flour*
> *1 tablespoon salt*
> *½ cup sugar*
> *1 teaspoon baking soda*
> *8 tablespoons (1 stick) unsalted butter, cold*
>   *and cut into pieces*
> *1 cup milk, plus additional*

Heat oven to 325°. Spray baking sheets with pan spray and dust lightly with flour.

In a bowl, sift together flour, salt, sugar, and baking soda. Cut in butter until mixture resembles coarse cornmeal. Make a well in the center and pour in milk. Mix well with a fork to make a soft dough. Add additional milk, if necessary.

Transfer dough to a well-floured surface and roll out to about ⅛ inch thick. Cut into desired shapes (scalloped rectangles, triangles, or rounds, for example) and transfer to baking sheets. Bake for 10–12 minutes, until golden brown. Brush off excess flour when cool.

Makes 10–12 dozen crackers

Generations Cheese-Stuffed Bread

Our family collects recipes from each other during reunions and "potlucks," passing them down from generation to generation. This is the most popular recipe.

You can vary the flavor and eye appeal of these loaves by sprinkling the tops with sesame seeds, poppy seeds, coarse sea salt, or dehydrated garlic before baking.

FOR DOUGH

½ cup warm water
1 tablespoon sugar
5 teaspoons active dry yeast
5 cups bread flour
1 teaspoon baking powder
2 large eggs
1 teaspoon salt
8 tablespoons (1 stick) unsalted butter,
      melted
1 cup warm milk

FOR FILLING

8 ounces cream cheese
1 egg yolk
½ cup sugar
1 teaspoon vanilla extract

1 egg yolk beaten with 1 tablespoon water,
      for egg wash

For dough: In a small bowl, combine water, sugar, and yeast. Cover and let sit for 20 minutes, until foamy.

In a bowl, combine flour and baking powder.

In a separate bowl, stir together eggs, salt, butter, and milk. Add wet ingredients and yeast mixture to dry ingredients, mixing to make a dough.

Turn dough out onto floured surface and knead 20 minutes until smooth. Place dough in a well-greased bowl, turning to bring greased side up. Cover with a kitchen towel and let rise in a warm place until doubled, about 2 hours (1 hour if you use rapid-rise yeast). Punch dough down, cover with kitchen towel, and let rise again until almost doubled, about 40 minutes.

For filling: In a bowl, mix together cream cheese, egg yolk, sugar, and vanilla until smooth. Set aside.

Cut dough into 4 pieces. On a floured surface, roll a piece into a rectangular/oval shape about ¼ inch thick. Spread one-quarter of the filling over dough with a spatula. Leave about 1½ inches of dough on far edge and sides without filling. Roll gently from long side (3–3½ turns) as you would a jelly roll to form a loaf. Gently seal both ends of rolled dough by folding the ends under and pinching them closed at the seams. Gently continue rolling to tighten and completely seal the seam and shape the loaf to uniform thickness from end to end. Set seam side down on baking sheet. Repeat this procedure with the other pieces of dough and place 2 loaves 4 inches apart on each baking sheet.

Heat oven to 300°. Let loaves rise 30 minutes. Brush top of dough with egg wash to give the bread its golden color. At this point, you may garnish loaves (see headnote). Bake for 30 minutes.

Makes 4 loaves

Puffed Cheese Rolls

The finished breads look like puffed pastries or éclairs. They tend to collapse when removed from heat prematurely. Turn oven off and leave in oven to produce crispier and firmer puffed rolls. The centers will remain hollow, soft, and cheesy.

Unused batter keeps for weeks if well covered under refrigeration. To reuse batter, whisk until thick again before filling muffin tins. Sweet and bitter yucca flour can be purchased from any Brazilian store and many specialty markets.

Do not be alarmed by the amount of salt and oil needed in the recipe. It gets absorbed and blends well with the yucca flour.

> 2¼ cups milk
> 2 cups plus 2 tablespoons grated Parmesan cheese, or 2 (6-ounce) packages
> 2½ cups corn oil
> 5 large eggs
> 1¼ tablespoons salt
> 2⅓ cups yucca sweet flour
> 1¾ cups yucca bitter flour

Heat oven to 375°. Spray mini-muffin tins with pan spray.

In a saucepan, heat milk to a simmer. Do not boil.

In a food processor, grind Parmesan to extra-fine granules. Add corn oil and process until smooth. With processor on, add eggs, one at a time, and process until mixture becomes very thick. Transfer cheese-egg mixture to the bowl of a stand mixer fitted with the whisk. Beat at slow speed while adding heated milk in a steady stream. Add salt. Continue beating on medium speed for 3 minutes.

In a large bowl, carefully combine sweet and bitter yucca flours and gradually add to liquid mixture. Mixture will be lumpy at this point. Beat at high speed for 5 minutes, or until batter has the consistency of a thick pancake batter.

Fill muffin cups to the rim. Bake for 20 minutes. Serve piping hot.

Makes about 7 dozen cheese rolls

President (41) and Mrs. Bush dined at a very famous Brazilian restaurant in Houston with their neighbors Jack and Bobbie Fitch. They came home raving about the restaurant's carved-at-your-table meat entrées and how they favored the cheese rolls that complemented their meals. Mr. Fitch came over a few days later and handed me the recipe for the cheese rolls, which he had acquired from the restaurant. The listed ingredients yielded 92 dozen, with no clear procedure on how to make the rolls with the exception of the baking time and oven temperature. I tested the recipe and broke it down to yield 4 dozen rolls, but the finished product did not come out right.

Mrs. Bush was to attend a celebration in Rio de Janeiro, and she said she would talk to her friends down there about the recipe. She came home from Brazil with two more variations for the Brazilian cheese rolls. As I compared the three recipes, I found that each of the newer recipes required more oil and more salt than the restaurant's recipe called for. My doubts led me to call the manager of the famous restaurant, and he immediately arranged a meeting between the restaurant chef and me the same day. I never met a friendlier group of people. They were the tops. They showed me the whole process, from the very beginning to the taste test. The rolls were indeed superb.

Every chance I get, from then on, I make these mouthwatering cheese rolls to complement salads and main courses. I have served the rolls to guests at the Bush residence in Houston, at the Presidential Library residence at Texas A&M, and at Walker's Point. For any dinner event at Walker's Point that requires a caterer's assistance, Mrs. Bush always asks me to provide the cheese rolls along with our own Walker's Point dessert selections. Everything else would always be provided by their favorite caterer, Foster's Downeast Clambake from York Harbor, Maine, for this event. Kevin Tacy, the caterer/proprietor, gladly obliges because at the end of each event, he trades me all his extra steamed lobsters and steamed clams for my extra cheese rolls. What a trade-off!

Special thanks to our Brazilian friends in Houston for this recipe, which now yields 7 dozen mini-cheese rolls.

Favorite Butterhorns

1 cake fresh yeast (do not substitute dry yeast)
½ cup plus 2 teaspoons sugar
1½ cups milk
1½ cups (3 sticks) unsalted butter, at room temperature
1 teaspoon salt
3 large eggs
5½ cups all-purpose flour

In a small bowl, crumble yeast and mix together with 2 teaspoons sugar. Set aside.

In a saucepan, scald milk and remove from heat.

In a large bowl, combine 1 cup butter, ½ cup sugar, and salt. Add scalded milk and stir until butter is melted. Add eggs, one at a time, beating well after each addition. Add yeast mixture. Add 3 cups flour and mix well. Add the remaining 2½ cups flour gradually, ½ cup at a time, mixing well after each addition.

Dough will be sticky. Cover bowl with plastic wrap and let rise in warm place until it doubles in size. Punch down. Cover and refrigerate overnight.

Grease a baking sheet.

Punch down dough and divide into 4 parts. Work with one part at a time, refrigerating remaining parts until ready for use. On a floured surface, roll into 12-inch circle. Spread with 2 tablespoons of softened butter. Cut circle into 8 wedges. Roll each wedge from wide end to point. Curve into crescent shape and place on baking sheet. Cover loosely with plastic wrap and let rise at room temperature for 2 hours.

Heat oven to 375°.

Bake for 15 minutes or until golden. Dough will keep in refrigerator for 2 weeks.

Makes 32 butterhorns

Homemade Philippine Rolls

Romeo Cruz, one of the seven Navy Culinary Specialists assigned to the Vice President's House during Bush's first term as Vice President, was the designated baker. This is his version of the rolls.

½ cup warm water
2 packages active dry yeast
2 tablespoons plus 1 teaspoon sugar
1 (12-ounce) can evaporated milk
4 tablespoons butter
3 egg yolks
1 teaspoon salt
8 cups bread flour
1 egg white beaten with 1 tablespoon water, for egg wash
2 cups superfine bread crumbs (see Note)

In a small bowl, combine water, yeast, and 1 teaspoon sugar. Stir to dissolve. Set aside until bubbly.

In a saucepan, heat milk until it begins to simmer. Remove from heat. Add butter and stir until melted. Set aside and cool to lukewarm.

In a large bowl, beat egg yolks, 2 tablespoons sugar, and salt together until smooth and pale in color. Gradually add the warm milk-butter mixture into the egg mixture. At this point, adjust sweetness by adding more sugar by the half teaspoon, if desired. Stir in the yeast mixture.

Add 4 cups of flour and mix by hand. Add remaining flour, 1 cup at a time, and mix by hand after each addition until dough can be handled easily. Transfer sticky dough to a work surface dusted lightly with flour and knead until dough is smooth and elastic and no longer sticks to the lightly floured work surface. Form dough into a ball and transfer to a greased bowl, turning to bring greased side up. Cover with a kitchen towel. Let rise in a warm place until doubled in size, about 1½ hours (see Note).

Punch down to deflate dough and knead to form a ball again. Cover with a towel and let dough rise again until almost doubled in volume, about 40 minutes.

Grease a baking sheet.

Divide dough into 3 equal pieces. Shape each into a ball and set aside on a well-floured work surface. Roll each piece into an even log about 12 inches long. Cut into 12 equal pieces and shape each into smaller balls. Brush each ball with egg wash.

Sprinkle with superfine bread crumbs and shake off excess. Arrange in rows on greased baking sheet, about 1 inch apart. Repeat with remaining dough and bread crumbs.

Place sheet pan in a warm oven and allow ball-shaped dough to ferment again, about 25 minutes. Remove from oven.

Heat oven to 425°.

Bake for 12–15 minutes, or until golden brown.

Makes about 36 rolls

Note: For superfine bread crumbs, start with about 3 cups dry bread crumbs. Shake crumbs through fine sieve, leaving coarser crumbs in sieve. Measure out 2 cups of the finest crumbs.

I let dough rise in the oven. If I have not used the oven earlier in the day, I turn it to a high temperature and let it heat for about 2 minutes. Then I turn the oven off and open the oven door. To check if dough has doubled, press down into it with two fingers. If the dough bounces back slightly, it needs to rise more; if your fingers leave an indentation, the dough is ready.

Chamorro Dinner Rolls

When I was stationed in Guam, one of the local residents, Mrs. Virginia Crisostomo, shared her version of this famous island recipe, Pan de Monay, *with me.*

2 (12-ounce) cans evaporated milk
2 cups sugar
1½ teaspoons salt

3 large eggs
2 packages active dry yeast
½ cup vegetable oil
¼ cup vodka
9 cups bread flour, sifted
1 egg beaten with 1 teaspoon water, for egg wash

In a small saucepan over low heat, warm canned milk, sugar, and salt, stirring until sugar is dissolved. Remove from heat and beat in eggs. Let cool to lukewarm. Sprinkle in yeast and stir to dissolve. Add oil and vodka. Set aside and allow liquid mixture to become bubbly.

Place flour in bowl of a stand mixer fitted with dough hook. With machine on low, blend in liquid mixture. When soft dough forms, increase speed to high and mix until dough becomes elastic and no longer sticks to the sides of the bowl, about 5 minutes.

Form dough into a ball and place in a greased bowl, turning to bring greased side up. Cover with a damp towel. Allow dough to rise in a warm place until double in size, about 1 hour (see Note, page 235).

Punch down, cover, and allow dough to rise again until almost double in size, about 1 hour. Punch dough and let rise again, for a total of 3 hours fermentation. Gather dough into a large ball. Divide dough evenly in two and work half of dough into a long log. Cut into golf ball–sized pieces. Grease a baking sheet and arrange balls of dough compactly. Repeat with remaining dough. Allow dough to rest 30 minutes before baking.

Heat oven to 425°.

Brush dough with egg wash. Bake for 18 minutes, until bottoms are an even golden brown. Remove from oven and allow rolls to cool. Cover rolls with plastic wrap while still slightly warm to soften crust.

Makes about 48 dinner rolls

CAKES, PIES, COOKIES, AND DESSERTS

Lemon Chiffon Cake • Soft Custard • Chocolate Chiffon Cake •
Buttermilk Layer Cake with Strawberry Cream • French Buttercream Frosting •
Sponge Cake • Chocolate Indulgence • Walker's Point Blueberry Pie •
Pecan Pie • Chocolate Pecan Pie • Blueberry Squares •
Chocolate Chip Cookies • Nutty Chocolate Chip Cookies • Ricky's Chocolate
Chips • Gingerbread Cookies • Lemon Bars • Oatmeal Lace Cookies •
Peanut Butter Cookies • Pecan Dainties • Pecan Tarts • Paula Rendon's
Sugar Cookies • Viennese Crescents • Apple Betty • Apple Crisp •
Baked Alaska • Simple Chocolate-Coffee Mousse • Chocolate-Coffee Crème
Brûlée Cheesecake • Chocolate Meringue Sundaes • Chocolate Soufflé •
Cream Puffs • Rich Custard Filling • Crème Brûlée • Crêpes Suzette •
Esponjosa (Caramel Soufflé) • Herman's Floating Island • Fruity Meringue Roll
on Sabayon Sauce • Baked Peaches Flambé • Paula's Pears in Wine
with Zabaglione Sauce • Meringue Bread Pudding • Raspberry Parfait

Oatmeal Lace Cookies

Lemon Chiffon Cake

1½ cups sugar
1 cup all-purpose flour
1 teaspoon baking powder
¼ teaspoon salt
4 egg yolks
½ cup vegetable oil
½ cup lemon juice
1 teaspoon vanilla extract
6 egg whites

Heat oven to 350°. Butter or coat with pan spray a 9 x 3-inch round cake pan. Dust with flour and tap out excess.

Sift 1 cup sugar, flour, baking powder, and salt together three times and set aside.

In a large bowl of an electric mixer, beat eggs yolks at high speed until pale in color. Turn machine to low and add oil, lemon juice, vanilla, and sifted dry ingredients. Turn speed up to high and beat 3 minutes, or until well combined.

In another large bowl, whip egg whites until soft peaks form. Gradually add remaining ½ cup sugar and continue to whip until whites are shiny and firm but not dry. Fold one-quarter of the whites into the egg yolk mixture, then scrape the egg yolk mixture into the whites, quickly folding to incorporate well.

Scrape batter into pan and bake for 25–30 minutes, or until edges pull away from the pan. Loosen cake by running a sharp knife around inside of pan. Invert onto cake rack. Invert again onto serving dish or round tray.

Serves 8

VARIATION

Filled Lemon Chiffon Cake

FOR FILLING

4 cups blueberries
¼ cup Chambord or liqueur of your choice
2 cups Soft Custard (recipe follows)
2 tablespoons light brown sugar

Follow master recipe for Lemon Chiffon Cake, baking cake in a Bundt cake pan coated with vegetable spray and dusted with flour. Allow cake to cool completely.

Meanwhile, in a medium bowl, macerate blueberries in Chambord.

Place cake on a serving plate. With a slotted spoon, carefully transfer berries to opening in the center of the cake. Top with Soft Custard spooned over the berries and drizzled down the sides of the cake. Sprinkle 1 tablespoon light brown sugar over the soft custard and caramelize with a portable torch. Repeat with another tablespoon sugar.

Soft Custard

6 egg yolks or 3 large eggs
⅓ cup sugar
½ teaspoon salt
2¼ cups whole milk
1½ teaspoons vanilla extract

In a large bowl, beat egg yolks lightly. Add sugar and salt and beat until well blended. Set aside.

In a small saucepan, scald milk. Whisking vigorously, pour hot milk into eggs. Transfer milk-egg mixture to double boiler or set bowl over pot of simmering water and cook, stirring, until custard thickens. Remove from heat and blend in vanilla.

Makes 2 cups

Sitting from left to right: Aunt Nancy Ellis, President George W. Bush, his sister, Doro, and me, standing behind the President.

Every year, as his birthday approached, the President would ask Mom and Dad, "Are you going to give me a surprise party?" Each year, Mr. and Mrs. Bush always came up with a "surprise" party. Even at fifty-five and the 43rd President of the United States, in 2001, he asked his mother the same question. We accommodated him with a party during his first and second presidential birthday celebration held at Walker's Point. My share of the surprise was his birthday cake—a Baked Alaska Cake with the presidential seal.

Another "surprise" party given to #43 on his fifty-sixth birthday on July 6, 2002, at Walker's Point. His party was attended by twenty-six immediate relatives. The dinner menu consisted of Chicken Combo, Spinach Soufflé filled with buttered baby carrots, Nutty Rice Pilaf, Puffed Cheese Rolls, and, for dessert, a Chocolate Chiffon Cake I decorated with a likeness of the First Dog, Barney.

The President compares the real Barney to his replica on top of the cake.

Chocolate Chiffon Cake

1½ cups sugar
1 cup all-purpose flour
¾ cup unsweetened cocoa powder
2 teaspoons baking powder
1 teaspoon baking soda
¼ teaspoon salt
4 egg yolks
¾ cup vegetable oil
½ cup water
1 teaspoon vanilla extract
6 egg whites

Heat oven to 350º. Butter and flour a 9 x 3-inch round cake pan.

Sift 1 cup sugar, flour, cocoa powder, baking powder, baking soda, and salt together three times. Set aside.

In the bowl of an electric mixer, beat egg yolks at medium speed until pale yellow. Reduce to low speed; beat in oil, water, and vanilla. Gradually add sifted dry ingredients and, when almost fully incorporated, turn speed to medium and beat until well combined.

In another large bowl, whip egg whites until soft peaks form. Gradually add ½ cup sugar to egg whites and continue whipping until shiny and firm but not stiff.

With a rubber scraper, fold one-quarter of the egg whites into the chocolate mixture, then scrape the chocolate mixture back into the remaining egg whites, gently folding until completely incorporated.

Pour batter into cake pan and bake for 30 minutes, or until edges pull away from pan. Cool on a rack.

Serves 8

VARIATION

Filled Chocolate Chiffon Cake: Bake in buttered and floured Bundt cake pan and fill center with assorted diced and sliced fruits (kiwi, cantaloupe, honeydew, strawberries, pineapple, papaya, bananas) and top with Soft Custard (page 239).

The staff members at the Vice President's Office invited the Beach Boys to join and celebrate the fifty-eighth birthday of then–Vice President George Herbert Walker Bush. A large tent was erected to accommodate more than three hundred guests at the Vice President's residence at the U.S. Naval Observatory Circle, Massachusetts Avenue, Washington, D.C. The Beach Boys' performance was superb and was the highlight of the evening. During a break, Vice President Bush was summoned onstage. Herman Capati and I walked in to present the Buttermilk Layer Cake, which I had decorated with the vice presidential seal in French Buttercream. It signaled the singing of "Happy Birthday," joined by everyone in attendance.

Buttermilk Layer Cake with Strawberry Cream

FOR CAKE

3½ cups all-purpose flour
4 teaspoons baking powder
1 teaspoon baking soda
½ teaspoon salt
1 cup (2 sticks) unsalted butter, softened
1½ cups sugar
8 egg yolks
2 cups buttermilk

FOR STRAWBERRY CREAM

1 pint strawberries, halved
¾ cup sugar
¼ cup water
1 cup light cream
4 egg yolks
2 teaspoons unflavored gelatin
2 tablespoons cold water

FOR MERINGUE

½ cup sugar
¼ cup water
4 egg whites
⅛ teaspoon cream of tartar

TO FINISH

2 pints strawberries, stemmed and cut into
    thin slices (set aside 8 berries with stems,
    for garnish)

For cake: Heat oven to 350º. Coat a 9 x 3-inch round cake pan with pan spray and dust with flour. Tap out excess flour. Set aside.

Sift flour, baking powder, baking soda, and salt together twice.

In a large bowl of an electric mixer, beat butter and sugar at medium speed, until fluffy. Add egg yolks, one at a time, beating well after each addition. Turn speed to low and, beginning and ending with the dry ingredients, add dry ingredients alternately with the buttermilk. Pour batter into cake pan; level surface. Bake for about 45 minutes, or until tester comes out clean. Invert cakes onto 10-inch cake board. Cool completely on cake racks.

For strawberry cream: In a large saucepan, bring strawberries, ¼ cup sugar, and water to a boil. Lower heat and cook until berries are very soft, about 15 minutes. Cool. Transfer to a blender and puree. Strain and measure. Mixture should yield no more than ¾ cup. Return mixture to saucepan. Add cream and bring to a boil.

In a large bowl of an electric mixer, beat egg yolks and ½ cup sugar on high speed until thick. Reduce speed to medium; slowly pour in hot strawberry mixture and beat until combined.

In a separate saucepan, dissolve gelatin in cold water. Heat until gelatin is completely dissolved; add to hot cream and continue beating. Strain and set aside.

For meringue: In a saucepan over medium-high heat, combine sugar and water. Cook until bubbly; do not stir.

In the bowl of an electric mixer, whip egg whites at low speed until frothy. Add cream of tartar, increase speed to medium-high, and beat to soft peaks. Still beating, pour the boiling syrup into the egg whites, avoiding the whisk. When the syrup is completely incorporated, increase speed to high and continue to beat until the whites are nice and shiny, forming firm peaks. Fold a little meringue into the strawberry cream to lighten it. Fold lightened cream into remaining meringue. Cover and chill for 2 hours, or until thick enough to spread.

To finish: Set aside 1 cup strawberry cream, covered, in the refrigerator. Fold strawberry slices into remaining strawberry cream.

Slice off mounded top of cake. Cut cake into three even layers.

Lightly coat a round tray with pan spray; center one layer on tray. Spread half the strawberry cream over the first layer. Carefully set second layer on top. Spread remaining strawberry cream over top of second layer. Carefully set third layer on top. Refrigerate until firm, 2–3 hours, or overnight.

Invert cake onto a flat serving plate and carefully lift off tray (applying a hot towel to tray will help release it). Spoon on reserved strawberry cream and spread evenly over top of cake. Refrigerate until ready to serve.

Partially slice the 8 reserved strawberries, leaving stem ends intact; spread strawberries into fans. Arrange on top of cake, spacing so each slice will be topped by a fan.

Serves 8

Note: I also use French Buttercream Frosting (recipe follows) to frost this cake.

French Buttercream Frosting

5 large eggs
2 cups sugar
½ cup water
1 tablespoon light corn syrup
1¼ pounds (5 sticks) unsalted butter, softened and cut into pieces
1 tablespoon vanilla extract
Pinch of salt

In the bowl of an electric mixer fitted with the whisk, beat eggs until very light and pale yellow.

In a small saucepan over medium heat, combine sugar, water, and corn syrup and cook until mixture reaches the soft-ball stage (235° on a candy thermometer); do not stir.

Turn the mixer to high speed. In a slow and steady stream pour syrup into the bowl of beaten eggs, making sure that none of the syrup falls on the whisk attachment. Whip until fluffy and mixer bowl is just warm (test temperature by placing palm against the outside bottom of the bowl). Beat in the butter, piece by piece, then beat about 2 minutes, or until smooth and silky. Stir in vanilla and salt. Use immediately or cover with plastic and refrigerate for up to 4 days. Bring chilled buttercream to room temperature and beat until smooth before using.

Sponge Cake

5 egg yolks
1¼ cups sugar
¼ cup boiling water or coffee
1 tablespoon lemon juice
1 cup cake flour (sift before measuring)
1½ teaspoons baking powder
¼ teaspoon salt
5 egg whites

Heat oven to 350°.

In the bowl of an electric mixer fitted with the whisk, beat egg yolks on medium speed until very light and pale yellow in color. Gradually add sugar and beat until creamy. Turn machine to low speed and add hot water or coffee. Return to medium speed and beat for 2 minutes. Allow batter to cool slightly, then beat in lemon juice.

Sift together cake flour, baking powder, and salt. Gradually add dry ingredients to the egg yolk mixture. Stir for 2 minutes, or until well blended.

In a separate mixing bowl, whip egg whites until stiff but not dry. Fold egg whites lightly into batter.

Pour batter into an ungreased 9-inch tube pan and bake for 45 minutes.

Cool completely before removing from pan.

Serves 12

Chocolate Indulgence

FOR CAKE

1¼ cups cake flour
1 cup sugar
½ teaspoon baking powder
½ teaspoon baking soda
¼ teaspoon salt
⅓ cup water
½ cup low-fat sour cream
1 teaspoon vanilla extract
1 large egg, beaten
3 tablespoons unsalted butter, softened
3 ounces unsweetened chocolate, melted

FOR FILLING

½ cup heavy cream
4 ounces bittersweet chocolate, chopped
2 tablespoons seedless strawberry preserves
¼ teaspoon vanilla extract

TO ASSEMBLE

3 tablespoons seedless strawberry preserves, melted
10–12 whole strawberries, rinsed and hulled

FOR MOUSSE

12 ounces white chocolate, finely chopped
4 tablespoons water
1 tablespoon vanilla extract
2 cups heavy cream, well chilled

For cake: Heat oven to 350º. Grease and flour a 9-inch round cake pan, tapping out excess flour. Set aside.

In a small bowl stir together flour, sugar, baking powder, baking soda, and salt. Set aside.

In a larger bowl, combine water, sour cream, vanilla, and egg; mix well. Stir in butter and chocolate. Add dry ingredients and beat with electric mixer on low speed for 1 minute. Beat on high speed for 3 minutes, scraping bowl frequently. Pour into pan.

Bake for 30–35 minutes, or until tester inserted in center comes out clean. Cool on wire rack.

For filling: In a small saucepan over low heat, heat cream. Place chocolate in double boiler over hot, not simmering, water. Pour heated cream over chocolate, stirring gently until melted and smooth. Remove cream-chocolate mixture from heat. Add preserves and vanilla and stir until blended. Cover and chill to thicken.

To assemble: Cut top from cake layer so cake is ¾ inch thick. Fit cake layer into 9-inch springform pan, pressing gently with hand to fit snugly. Brush with melted preserves.

GROOM'S CAKE

This is George P. Bush's groom's cake, which I made for his wedding on August 7, 2004, to Mandi Williams in Kennebunkport, Maine. President and Mrs. Bush asked me to create a groom's cake for their first grandson—the oldest among their fourteen grandchildren, son of Florida Governor Jeb and Columba Bush—to be decorated with a theme of ringed horseshoes. The stake with three horseshoes was made out of Gingerbread Cookies (page 260) coated with chocolate icing. The cake was Buttermilk Layer Cake (page 244). The catered reception was held at one of the famous local restaurants, Stripers, and attended by more than two hundred guests. The cake was displayed right next to the tables occupied by George P. Bush's senior members' side of the family, and they went into raptures over the cake that summer.

Cut strawberries in vertical halves of uniform size. Arrange strawberries, pointed end up, around circumference of pan, placing cut sides firmly against inside of pan. Carefully pour filling into pan, spreading evenly to touch bases of the strawberries while holding them in place. Chill until firm.

For mousse: Place chocolate, water, and vanilla in a double boiler over hot but not simmering water. Stir constantly until chocolate is melted and smooth. Remove pan and cool to lukewarm (about 85°).

In a bowl, whip heavy cream until soft peaks form.

Carefully fold cream into chocolate, until just barely combined. Mousse will appear soft, but it sets quickly. Immediately pour over filling, covering strawberries completely.

WEDDING CAKES

During my military service in the U.S. Navy as a Steward to Mess Management Specialist and now known as Culinary Specialist, I gained dexterity in many trades in the hospitality services. Along with ice carving, butter sculpting, and vegetable carving and garnitures came cake decorating. Even though I have not received any formal instructions to acquire these specialty skills, my on-the-job training has sufficed. I was one of many who has been lucky to be surrounded by skillful and talented Navy Culinary Specialists and nurtured by their skills. My cake decorating has usually been limited to birthday cakes and ceremonial cakes, but it became why-the-heck-not for wedding cakes as well. While at Walker's Point, I was given the chance to prepare wedding cakes for two brides who were formerly aides to Mrs. Bush, Quincy Hicks and Brooke Sheldon, and another for Wendy and Diego. Wendy is the daughter of Craig and Debbie Stapleton. Craig was the U.S. ambassador to Prague in 2003 and U.S. ambassador to France in 2005.

Smooth top of mousse by leveling with a spatula. Refrigerate, covered, 4–6 hours, until set. Unmold gently.

Serves 12–16

Walker's Point Blueberry Pie

Avoid doubling the filling ingredients if you plan to make more than one pie. Always prepare each filling in its own mixing bowl. That way, each pie will not only have the same amount of filling but will also have the same taste and consistency.

FOR CRUST

2 cups all-purpose flour
$\frac{1}{2}$ teaspoon salt
$\frac{2}{3}$ cup vegetable shortening, chilled
4 tablespoons ice water

FOR FILLING

4 cups blueberries, washed, drained, and dried completely on paper towels
1 tablespoon lemon juice
2 tablespoons all-purpose flour
$\frac{1}{8}$ teaspoon salt
1 cup sugar
$1\frac{1}{2}$ tablespoons unsalted butter, cut into small pieces

---

PIES

Regardless of the many different pies served and created around the world, I can only reveal three pies in this book. This is not because they are the only ones I know how to make, but these three pies are the only ones I serve to the entire Bush family and their guests. I always make sure we have one or two pies in the freezer on standby, just in case they ask for it. Top with ice cream or whipped cream—you can never go wrong.

For crust: In a bowl, use a fork to stir flour and salt together. Cut in shortening with a pastry blender until mixture resembles very coarse cornmeal.

With a fork, stir in the ice water, 1 tablespoon at a time, until pastry holds together. Shape into a flat disk. Wrap in wax paper and chill for 30 minutes.

Heat oven to 425º.

Divide the dough in half, one slightly larger, and gently shape each into a ball. On a lightly floured surface, roll out larger ball into a 13-inch-thick circle, about ⅛ inch thick. Roll crust onto rolling pin and then unroll it over a 9-inch pie plate. (If you prefer, fold the crust in half, lift, and place it in the pie plate.) Fit the pastry loosely into pie plate. Do not trim edges; allow crust to hang over sides of pie plate. Set aside.

For filling: In a bowl, combine berries, lemon juice, flour, salt, and sugar and blend well. Pour berries into pastry-lined pie plate. Dot top with butter.

Dust working surface with more flour, as needed, and roll out the smaller ball. With sharp knife, cut a few slits in center of crust. Center top crust over berries. Gently fold overhang under bottom crust. Pinch a high decorative edge. Bake for 40 minutes, or until crust is nicely browned and juices begin to bubble through slits in crust. Serve warm.

Serves 8

Paula Rendon's Blueberry Pies

Pecan Pie

This recipe was shared by Paula Rendon. When Neil Bush is among the diners, I make sure he gets a piece of pie—even when I have other desserts planned for that meal. For Neil, the meal is not complete unless he finishes it with a piece of pecan pie. Amazingly, he can also detect if the pie is made using Paula's recipe or commercially purchased.

FOR CRUST

1¼ cups all-purpose flour
¾ teaspoon salt
6½ tablespoons vegetable shortening
3–4 tablespoons ice water

FOR FILLING

1 cup sugar
½ teaspoon salt
4 tablespoons unsalted butter, melted
½ cup light corn syrup
3 large eggs, well beaten
¼ cup rum (dark or white)
1 cup pecan chunks
Whole pecans (optional)

For crust: In a bowl, use a fork to stir together flour and salt. Cut in shortening with a pastry blender until mixture resembles very coarse cornmeal.

With a fork, stir in the ice water, 1 tablespoon at a time, until pastry holds together. Shape into a flat disk, wrap in wax paper, and chill for 30 minutes.

Heat oven to 375°.

On a lightly floured surface, roll pastry out into a 13-inch circle, about ⅛ inch thick. Roll crust onto rolling pin and unroll it over a 9-inch pie plate. (If you prefer, fold crust in half, lift, and place in pie plate.) Fit pastry loosely into pie plate. Pinch a high decorative edge. Set aside.

For filling: In a bowl, beat sugar, salt, butter, and corn syrup together with an electric mixer. Add eggs and rum. Stir in pecan chunks thoroughly. Pour into pastry-lined pie plate. Arrange whole pecans decoratively on top of filling, if desired. Bake for 45 minutes, or until filling is set and pastry is browned. Serve warm.

Serves 8

Chocolate Pecan Pie

Paula told me a funny story about how she introduced this recipe to the Bush family for the first time. She found the recipe in an airlines magazine and secretly prepared the pie. She wrapped and froze it for future use. Reverend Billy Graham and Cardinal Law of Boston came for dinner one night and, without giving notice to Mrs. Bush, Paula heated up the pie for dessert. Warily eyeing the pie and having doubts about its flavor, Mrs. Bush blurted out, "We've never served chocolate pecan pie in this house." President Bush asked Paula if she could top his piece with vanilla ice cream. After everyone consumed the dessert, the Reverend Graham called Paula in and whispered to request another slice. The cardinal followed suit. Mrs. Bush gladly accepted the overwhelming and heavenly approvals.

FOR CRUST

1¼ cups all-purpose flour
¾ teaspoon salt
6½ tablespoons vegetable shortening, chilled
3–4 tablespoons ice water

FOR FILLING

2 ounces unsweetened chocolate
2 tablespoons unsalted butter
3 large eggs, beaten
½ cup sugar
¾ cup light corn syrup
¾ cup pecan chunks

For crust: In a bowl, use a fork to stir together flour and salt. Cut in shortening with a pastry blender until mixture resembles very coarse cornmeal.

With a fork, stir in the ice water, 1 tablespoon at a time, until pastry holds together. Shape into a flat disk, wrap in wax paper, and chill for 30 minutes.

Heat oven to 375°.

On a lightly floured surface, roll pastry out into a 13-inch circle, about ⅛ inch thick. Roll crust onto rolling pin and unroll it over a 9-inch pie plate. (If you prefer, fold crust in half, lift, and place in pie plate.) Fit pastry loosely into pie plate. Pinch a high decorative edge. Set aside.

For filling: In a bowl set over simmering water, melt chocolate and butter. Remove from heat and add eggs, sugar, and corn syrup; beat well. Mix in pecans. Pour into pastry-lined pie plate. Bake for 45 minutes, or until filling is set and pastry is browned. Serve warm.

Serves 8

Blueberry Squares

This recipe was shared by Carolyn Broad of Kennebunk, Maine. Carolyn started as a dedicated volunteer worker at the Walker's Point office of George Bush during his tenure a President. She has kept in touch not only with the Bush family but also with all members of the staff, past and present.

¾ cup sugar
1 large egg
1 teaspoon lemon extract
½ teaspoon grated nutmeg
Dash of salt
¾ cup whole milk
1¾ cups all-purpose flour, plus additional for dusting
2 teaspoons baking powder

COOKIES

Of all my cookie recipes, my favorites have always been Chocolate Chip Cookies, Viennese Crescents, Oatmeal Lace Cookies, Pecan Tarts, and Nutty Chocolate Chip Cookies. This is not only because of their popularity but also because these particular cookies bring back sweet and joyful memories.

Going back to the time of Mr. Bush's vice presidency, Mrs. Bush entertained a group of Brownie Scouts at the Vice President's House. She started with her usual welcome speech, adding information about the house and its historical significance.

She noticed many of the Brownies weren't paying much attention to her speech because Orlando Frilles and I unknowingly distracted them as we set the table with drinks and assorted cookies. She hurriedly finished her speech, saying, "This house has a huge kitchen, which is located in the basement of this three-story house, home of the Vice President of the United States. All food prepared from the basement is brought up to this floor by using the dumbwaiter." She then invited everyone to help themselves to the cookies. As I was passing drinks to the little girls, one of them tugged my pants and said, "Mister, I don't care if you're dumb; your cookies are good anyway."

---

4 tablespoons unsalted butter, melted, or corn oil
2 cups blueberries

Heat oven to 400º.

In a bowl, beat sugar, egg, lemon extract, nutmeg, and salt together until smooth. Add milk, flour, and baking powder and stir until well incorporated. Stir in melted butter.

Pick over blueberries, removing stems and discarding wilted ones. Rinse and dry with paper towels. In a bowl, dust blueberries generously with flour. Fold flour-dusted blueberries into batter. Pour into an 8 x 8-inch pan. Bake for 30–35 minutes, until golden brown and bubbly. Allow baked blueberries to cool to room temperature before slicing into squares.

Makes 16 squares

Chocolate Chip Cookies

This recipe was shared by Mrs. Patsy Caulkins, Mrs. Bush's friend. We make these cookies by the hundreds, freeze most of them, and fill the cookie jars every morning. The jars are usually empty before dinner. Mr. Bush occasionally crams a dozen cookies in his briefcase before he leaves for long trips aboard Air Force Two and Air Force One.

1 cup (2 sticks) unsalted butter
1 cup granulated sugar
1 cup brown sugar, packed
2 large eggs
2 cups all-purpose flour
1 teaspoon baking soda
1 teaspoon salt
2 cups instant oatmeal
2 teaspoons vanilla extract
1 (12-ounce) package semisweet
    chocolate chips

Heat oven to 350°.

In the bowl of an electric mixer, cream butter and sugars. Add eggs and beat to mix.

In another bowl, sift flour, baking soda, and salt together. Add dry ingredients to wet. Add oatmeal, vanilla, and chocolate chips and stir to combine.

Drop by heaping teaspoonfuls on ungreased cookie sheets, allowing 2 inches between cookies. Bake for 10 minutes. Loosen from cookie sheets immediately after removing from oven. Transfer to cooling rack.

Makes 5–6 dozen cookies

Nutty Chocolate Chip Cookies

This recipe was shared by Winnie Palmer, late wife of the famous golf champion, Arnold Palmer, a dear friend of the Bush family for more than twenty years.

Winnie Palmer sent Barbara Bush this recipe based on a story she heard about a lady who asked a famous department store for a recipe. They wouldn't give it to the lady for free, but sold it to her for "two fifty." When she got her bill, it was $250 not $2.50. They would not adjust the bill, saying that was what they charged for the recipe. So she distributed the recipe for free to anyone who wanted it! Almonds, cashews, pecans, walnuts, or any combination are widely used.

> 1 cup (2 sticks) unsalted butter, softened
> 1 cup granulated sugar
> 1 cup brown sugar, packed
> 2 large eggs
> 1 teaspoon vanilla extract
> 2½ cups oatmeal
> 2 cups all-purpose flour, sifted
> ½ teaspoon salt
> 1 teaspoon baking powder
> 1 teaspoon baking soda
> 1 (12-ounce) package semisweet chocolate chips
> 1 (4-ounce) bar Hershey's milk chocolate, grated
> 1½ cups chopped walnuts

Heat oven to 375°.

In a bowl, cream butter and sugars until creamy. Add eggs and vanilla; mix well. Set aside.

Place oatmeal in a blender and grind to a fine powder. Add gradually to sugar-egg mixture, along with flour, salt, baking powder, and baking soda; stir to combine. Add chocolate chips, grated chocolate, and nuts.

Roll into golf ball–sized balls for large cookies; use 1 heaping teaspoon for smaller cookies, and place 2 inches apart on ungreased cookie sheets. Bake for 10 minutes.

Makes 2–6 dozen cookies

Ricky's Chocolate Chips

Mrs. Bush came home one day raving about yet another recipe. "Very special!" she said. It was given to her by the cook of Sandy and Nelson Doubleday, former owner of the New York Mets.

> 2 cups all-purpose flour, sift before measuring
> ½ teaspoon baking powder
> 1 teaspoon baking soda
> 1 teaspoon salt
> 1 cup (2 sticks) unsalted butter, melted
> ½ cup light brown sugar, packed
> ½ cup dark brown sugar, packed
> 1 cup granulated sugar
> 2 large eggs
> 1 teaspoon vanilla extract
> 1 (12-ounce) package semisweet chocolate chips

Heat oven to 350°. Grease cookie sheets.

In the bowl of an electric mixer, mix together flour, baking powder, baking soda, and salt. Gradually add butter, sugars, eggs, vanilla, and chocolate chips. Drop dough by the heaping teaspoonful, spacing evenly on cookie sheet. Bake for 5 minutes. Remove sheet from oven and smack it on a table or work surface (this flattens cookies nicely). Return to oven and bake for another 5 minutes.

Keeps best in freezer.

Makes 5 dozen cookies

Gingerbread Cookies

1½ teaspoons white vinegar
½ cup vegetable shortening
½ cup sugar
½ cup molasses
1 large egg, well beaten
3 cups all-purpose flour
½ teaspoon baking soda
¼ teaspoon salt
½ teaspoon ground cinnamon
½ teaspoon ground ginger

Heat oven to 375°. Grease cookie sheets.

In a saucepan, bring vinegar, shortening, sugar, and molasses to a boil. Cool. Add egg and stir well to blend.

In a bowl, sift together flour, baking soda, salt, cinnamon, and ginger. Add dry ingredients to wet. Mix well. Chill for at least 2 hours.

On a lightly floured surface, roll dough to about ⅛ inch for thin cookies, or ¼–½ inch thick for gingerbread houses. After cutting to desired shapes with cookie cutters, place shaped dough on greased cookie sheets. (Use a spatula to transfer cookies to cookie sheets to help keep the shapes.) Bake for 8–10 minutes. Allow cookies to cool completely before glazing or icing.

Makes about 36 cookies

The Vice Presidential Gingerbread House. I use the recipe for Gingerbread Cookies to make my annual gingerbread house for the holidays. I usually prepare double batches of dough. Roll, measure, cut, and bake shaped portions and continue mixing by batches until you have enough to build your gingerbread house. Use trimmings to patch up any breakage or occasional mistakes. Deformed and broken pieces of baked cookies are always a welcome treat in your cookie jar.

Lemon Bars

This recipe was shared by Sarah Walker, wife of Jimmy Walker, uncle of President George Herbert Walker Bush. The bars, rich and chewy, with lemony flavor, keep deliciously soft for days in a lightly covered jar.

> 1 cup plus 1 tablespoon all-purpose flour
> ¼ cup confectioners' sugar, plus additional for dusting
> ½ cup buttermilk
> 2 large eggs
> 1 cup granulated sugar
> ½ teaspoon baking powder
> 3–4 tablespoons lemon juice

Heat oven to 350°.

In a bowl, mix 1 cup flour, confectioners' sugar, and buttermilk together until soft and pliable. Pat dough down evenly into a 9-inch square pan. Bake for 20 minutes. Remove pan from oven. Leave oven on.

In another bowl, combine eggs, granulated sugar, 1 tablespoon flour, baking powder, and lemon juice to taste and beat well. Pour mixture onto the hot crust and return to oven. Bake for an additional 25 minutes. Dust top with confectioners' sugar when cool. Loosen sides with a sharp knife and cut into 16 squares.

Makes 16 bars

Oatmeal Lace Cookies

These are crisp, brown, shiny, and very thin cookies. Handle with care, for they are very brittle. They look like small doilies with many tiny holes. They may be shaped in any desired form while hot and pliable.

½ cup all-purpose flour
½ cup sugar
¼ teaspoon baking powder
½ cup oatmeal
2 tablespoons heavy cream
⅓ cup unsalted butter, melted
1 tablespoon vanilla extract
2 tablespoons light corn syrup

Heat oven to 375°.

In a mixing bowl, sift flour, sugar, and baking powder together.

Add other ingredients, one at a time, stirring well after each addition.

Drop slightly heaped teaspoons of dough onto nonstick cookie sheets, allowing 4 inches between cookies. Cookies will spread while being baked. (I pipe even portions of dough on a nonstick sheet pan using a filled pastry bag fitted with a large star tip.)

Bake for approximately 6 minutes (check after 4 minutes), or until lightly browned. Remove cookies from sheets while still warm; they tend to turn firm fast as they cool down. (Return to warm oven for easy handling.) They may be shaped and rolled like tiny cones, taco shells, or scalloped cups.

Makes about 48 cookies

Peanut Butter Cookies

This recipe was shared by Mrs. Grace Walker. President (41) Bush's Uncle Louis and Aunt Grace Walker have always been present during the many family events held at the Vice President's House, at the White House, at Camp David, at the George Bush Library, and at Walker's Point. Aunt Grace somehow managed to acquire recipes from the kitchen staff at every event she was invited to attend. She requested many recipes from me as well. Each time, I always complied to her every request. Occasionally, she would return the favor by trading with me some of her newly acquired recipes. "These are great recipes," she would whisper, her eyes darting around as if someone might catch her passing down secret documents, à la James Bond. Upon quick scrutiny, I would immediately recognize some of the recipes as ones I had shared with her during an earlier visit. Some would even bear my name. She's always such a very sweet and wonderful lady.

> ½ cup vegetable shortening
> ½ cup granulated sugar
> ½ cup brown sugar, packed
> ½ cup chunky peanut butter
> 1 large egg, beaten
> 1½ cups all-purpose flour
> 1 teaspoon baking soda
> ¼ teaspoon salt
> ½ teaspoon vanilla extract

Heat oven to 400°.

In a bowl, mix shortening, sugars, and peanut butter thoroughly. Add egg and mix to blend.

In another bowl, sift flour, baking soda, and salt together. Add to peanut butter mixture. Add vanilla and mix thoroughly. Chill at least 2 hours, or until firm.

Roll into golf ball–sized balls. Place on an ungreased baking sheet. Flatten with fingers gently. Bake for 10 minutes.

Makes 12 cookies

Pecan Dainties

These dainties were shared by Mrs. Mildred Kerr, a lifelong friend and movie-going partner of Mrs. Bush. They have known each other since 1940, and they lunch together in Houston every chance they get. Mrs. Kerr's husband, Baine, was the lawyer for Mr. Bush's company and later became president of Pennzoil.

> 1 egg white
> 1 cup light brown sugar, packed
> ½ cup pecan halves

Heat oven to 250°. Grease a cookie sheet.

In a bowl, beat egg white until stiff. Gradually add sugar, beating constantly. Stir in pecans. Drop from a teaspoon onto cookie sheet. Bake for 30 minutes. Turn oven off. Leave dainties in oven with door ajar for 10 minutes to hasten drying. Remove from cookie sheet and allow pecans to cool completely. Keeps well for a week in a tin cookie container.

Makes about 25 dainties

Pecan Tarts

The finished product will resemble miniature pecan pies. The yield will depend on how thick or thin you form the dough. I usually mold it as thin as I can without tearing the dough. Use your thumb and forefinger to push and raise edges higher than or level with the rims of the muffin tins.

FOR CRUST

8 ounces cream cheese, at room temperature
8 tablespoons (1 stick) unsalted butter, at room temperature
1½ cups all-purpose flour

FOR FILLING

5 large eggs
1 cup light brown sugar, packed
1 tablespoon unsalted butter, melted
Finely chopped pecans

For crust: In a bowl, mix cream cheese, butter, and flour together until soft and pliable. Form dough into balls about the size of your thumbnail. Press dough down against bottom and sides of the cups in mini-muffin tins to form small cups. Freeze for 1 hour.

Heat oven to 325°.

For filling: In a bowl, beat eggs, sugar, and butter until blended. Use a spoon to fill dough cups one-third full, stirring filling often.

Sprinkle chopped pecans on top to fill molds completely. Bake for 10–15 minutes, until golden brown.

Makes 36–42 tarts

Paula Rendon's Sugar Cookies

In her earlier years with the Bush family, Paula prepared this recipe and cut the cookies in different sizes and forms. Mrs. Bush loves to help decorate the cookies with colored sugar. Paula says the children also love to show their garniture skills—if she can keep them from eating the cookies first.

> ¾ cup vegetable shortening, softened
> 1 cup sugar
> 2 large eggs
> ½ teaspoon vanilla extract
> 2½ cups all-purpose flour, sifted
> 1 teaspoon baking powder
> 1 teaspoon salt

In a bowl mix shortening, sugar, eggs, and vanilla until smooth. Set aside.

Sift flour, baking powder, and salt. Stir into wet ingredients. Chill for at least 1 hour.

Heat oven to 400°.

On a floured surface, roll dough to ⅛ inch thick. Cut into desired shapes. Using a spatula, gently transfer to a baking sheet. Sprinkle with colored sugar. Bake for 6–8 minutes, or until cookies turn a delicate brown.

Makes about 4–5 dozen cookies

VARIATIONS

Lemon Sugar Cookies: Follow master recipe, substituting 2 teaspoons grated lemon zest and 1 teaspoon lemon juice for the vanilla.

Nutty Sugar Cookies: Follow master recipe, adding 1 cup finely chopped nuts.

Viennese Crescents

These finger-size crescent cookies are excellent at teatime or anytime. You may roll the cookies in prepared vanilla sugar or leave uncoated. I prefer to alternate coated and uncoated cookies on a serving platter for a nicer presentation.

You may vary the shapes by rolling dough into a log. Chill for at least 1 hour, slice into ½-inch-thick rounds, and bake.

FOR VANILLA SUGAR

¼ vanilla bean
1 cup confectioners' sugar

FOR COOKIES

1 cup walnut meats
½ cup all-purpose flour, sifted
1 cup (2 sticks) unsalted butter, melted

For vanilla sugar: Split vanilla bean in half lengthwise to expose seeds. Scrape seeds and save for another use. Finely mince pod. Pound it in a mortar or pulverize it in a blender with 1 tablespoon confectioners' sugar. Mix with remaining confectioners' sugar. Cover and let stand overnight.

For cookies: Heat oven to 350°.

In a food processor, coarsely chop walnuts to an almost pastelike consistency.

Transfer walnuts to a bowl. Add flour and butter and, with a wooden spoon, mix into a smooth dough.

Shape dough, about 1 teaspoon at a time, into small crescents. Bake on ungreased cookie sheets for 15 minutes, or until lightly browned.

Cool 1 minute and while still warm, roll cookies in vanilla sugar.

Makes about 36 crescents

Apple Betty

Serve warm, with whipped cream or ice cream.

> ¾ cup light brown sugar, packed
> ½ cup sifted all-purpose flour
> ½ cup rolled oats
> ¾ teaspoon ground cinnamon
> ¾ teaspoon grated nutmeg
> 4 tablespoons unsalted butter, softened
> 4 medium apples, cored, pared, and sliced
> ¼ cup orange juice

Heat oven to 375°. Spray an 8-inch square baking dish with pan spray.

In a bowl, blend the sugar, flour, oats, cinnamon, nutmeg, and butter together until crumbly. Set aside.

Spread one-third of crumbs over bottom of pan. Layer in half of the apple slices. Cover with another one-third of crumbs, then the remaining apple slices. Top with remaining crumbs. Level top. Drizzle orange juice evenly over the top.

Bake 30–35 minutes, or until apples are tender and topping is golden brown. Serve warm.

Serves 9

Apple Crisp

Apple Crisp and Apple Betty (page 269) are Marvin Bush's favorites since childhood. Every time Marvin comes to visit, either the Apple Crisp or Apple Betty is sure to be the dessert for the evening meal.

¾ cup dark brown sugar, packed firmly
½ cup sifted all-purpose flour
½ cup rolled oats
¾ teaspoon ground cinnamon
¾ teaspoon grated nutmeg
4 tablespoons unsalted butter, softened
4 medium apples, cored, pared, and sliced

Heat oven to 375°. Spray an 8-inch square baking dish with pan spray.

In a bowl, blend together sugar, flour, oats, cinnamon, nutmeg, and butter until crumbly.

Arrange apple slices in layers in baking dish. Spread crumbs over top of apple slices. Level top.

Bake for 30–35 minutes, or until apples are tender and topping is golden brown. Serve warm.

Serves 9

Baked Alaska

I make many variations when serving this dessert. The President George Bush (41) and Mrs. Barbara Bush gave a surprise birthday party for President George W. Bush (43) at Walker's Point on July 6, 2001. It was his very first birthday celebration as President of the United States. Twenty-three other family members attended the party. The dessert was Baked Alaska, but the bottom cake layer and ice cream was topped with a layer of cake covered with buttercream frosting, not meringue. I decorated the top layer with a presidential seal, while the borders and sides remained covered with meringue. Keep the bottom layer and ice cream in the freezer while you separately decorate the top layer with frosting. Assemble only when ready to serve by lifting the top layer cake over the ice cream. Cover edges with more meringue borders in your own piped designs. Finish by using a portable torch and lightly browning meringue to reveal the details of the design.

Robert Koch, the son of Doro and Bobby Koch, claims this cake is his very own favorite, but he calls it Cake and Ice Cream with Marshmallow Frosting.

> 2 quarts strawberry ice cream, slightly softened, plus additional
> 1 recipe Lemon Chiffon Cake or Chocolate Chiffon Cake (pages 238, 242)
>
> FOR MERINGUE
>
> 6 egg whites
> ½ teaspoon cream of tartar
> 1 cup superfine sugar

Pack 2 quarts ice cream into a 7-inch glass or stainless steel bowl. Freeze until solid.

Prepare cake, baking in a 12-inch round cake pan. Unmold onto an 11- or 12-inch cake board (available in kitchen supply stores) and trim off crust, so cake is slightly smaller than board. Cool completely.

When cool, cut top third from cake. (Poke toothpicks around edge of cake to guide your knife.) Scoop out some of the bottom layer, making a well about 8 inches wide. Press down with your hand to flatten bottom of well. Freeze bottom layer for 30 minutes; set top layer aside at room temperature.

Remove bottom layer and ice cream from freezer. With a spatula, loosen ice cream. Invert bowl over bottom cake layer, centering it within the rim. Remove bowl. Spread ice cream toward rim, adding additional ice cream to fill gaps, if necessary. Return to freezer while you make meringue.

Heat oven to 500º.

For meringue: In the bowl of an electric mixer fitted with the whisk, beat egg whites and cream of tartar until frothy. Still beating, gradually add sugar. Continue beating until stiff and glossy.

Scoop out some cake from middle of top layer, coming close to crust. Invert over ice cream and cover with plastic. Use plastic to help press top layer down evenly, until it meets bottom layer and covers ice cream completely. Remove plastic.

Cover cake with a thin layer of meringue, going all the way to the cake board to make a seal. Fill a pastry bag fitted with a star tip with remaining meringue. Pipe decorative designs around bottom of cake.

Place cake (on board) on baking sheet and place in oven for 3–5 minutes, until meringue is delicately browned. Place on dessert platter, board and all. With a portable torch, brown designs around bottom layer. Serve immediately.

Serves 8

Simple Chocolate-Coffee Mousse

FOR MOUSSE

1 pound semisweet chocolate chips
1 cup freshly brewed strong coffee
1 teaspoon vanilla extract
1 envelope unflavored gelatin
1 cup heavy cream

FOR TOPPING

1 cup heavy cream
¼ cup sugar
Berries, for garnish

For mousse: In a double boiler set over hot but not boiling water, melt chocolate. Add coffee and vanilla. Stir well. Remove top pan of double boiler from heat and stir in gelatin until dissolved. Let cool to room temperature.

In a bowl, whip cream to soft peaks. Fold half of the whipped cream into chocolate to lighten it, then fold lightened chocolate into remaining whipped cream.

Spoon mousse into 4–6 glasses and refrigerate until set.

For topping: In a bowl, beat cream to soft peaks. Add sugar and whip until smooth. With a pastry bag, pipe cream over mousse. Garnish with seasonal berries.

Serves 4–6

Chocolate-Coffee Crème Brûlée Cheesecake

FOR CRUST

3 cups crushed Oreo cookies (use a rolling pin)
8 tablespoons unsalted butter, softened

FOR CHEESECAKE FILLING

1½ pounds cream cheese, softened
1½ cups sugar
4 large eggs
1 teaspoon vanilla extract

FOR CHOCOLATE-COFFEE CRÈME BRÛLÉE

4 cups heavy cream
1 vanilla bean, split in half lengthwise
15 coffee beans
7 egg yolks
1 cup sugar
8 ounces semisweet chocolate

FOR SERVING

Strawberry fans (see page 246)

Heat oven to 350°. Wrap bottom and sides of a 10-inch springform pan tightly with aluminum foil.

For crust: Combine cookies and butter and pat over bottom and sides of the springform pan. Set aside.

For filling: In a bowl, beat cream cheese until light. Beat in sugar. Add eggs, one at a time, and beat until smooth. Stir in vanilla. Pour filling into springform pan. Place springform pan in larger pan, pour in about 1 inch hot water, and bake for 30 minutes. Remove from water bath to cool while you prepare chocolate-coffee crème brûlée.

For chocolate-coffee crème brûlée: In a saucepan, combine heavy cream and vanilla bean and bring to a boil. Remove from heat. Add coffee beans, cover, and allow to steep in hot cream for 1 hour. Strain cream. Discard coffee beans and scrape vanilla bean back into cream mixture in the saucepan. Discard bean pods. Set aside.

Heat oven to 300º.

In a large mixing bowl, beat yolks and sugar until pale yellow. Add a little cream mixture to the yolk mixture to lighten. Pour this mixture back into remaining cream in saucepan. Return saucepan to medium heat and cook, stirring constantly, until thick enough to coat the back of a spoon. Add chocolate and stir until melted. Remove from heat and gently pour over cheesecake. Return cheesecake to water bath and bake for 1½ hours, or until set. Remove from oven and let cool to room temperature. Refrigerate covered.

Release springform and remove cake. Cut into 10–12 wedges. Place each wedge onto a dessert plate. Garnish with strawberry fans.

Serves 10–12

Chocolate Meringue Sundaes

½ *cup chopped almonds*
4 egg whites
1 cup sugar
⅓ *cup Dutch-processed cocoa powder*

FOR SERVING

Ice cream
Quick Chocolate Sauce (page 213)

Heat oven to 350º. Line 2 cookie sheets with parchment. Draw 4 circles (3½ inches in diameter) on each sheet and set aside.

On a sheet pan, toast almonds in oven for 10–13 minutes, or until golden brown. Set aside to cool.

Reduce oven temperature to 250º.

In a bowl, whip egg whites to soft peaks. Gradually beat in sugar, one tablespoon at a time, until egg whites hold firm, glossy peaks. Sift cocoa powder over meringue and fold in, adding toasted almonds as you fold. Spoon meringue evenly onto circles and smooth with back of spoon. Bake for 1 hour in lower third of oven. Turn off heat and leave meringue in oven for 2 more hours. Cool meringues, and then gently peel off parchment.

Store in a well-sealed container until ready to use.

For serving: Top meringues with scoops of your favorite ice cream and drizzle top with Quick Chocolate Sauce.

Serves 4

Chocolate Soufflé

4 tablespoons unsalted butter
¼ cup all-purpose flour
¼ teaspoon salt
¾ cup whole milk
2 ounces unsweetened chocolate, chopped
3 egg yolks
½ cup sugar
3 egg whites
¼ teaspoon cream of tartar
Whipped cream, for serving
Toasted sliced almonds, for serving

Heat oven to 350°. Butter a 2-quart soufflé dish.

In a saucepan over medium heat, melt butter. Blend in flour and salt and cook until smooth and bubbly. Remove from heat and stir in milk. Add chocolate and return to heat and bring to a boil, stirring constantly. Boil 1 minute. Remove from heat. Set aside.

In a bowl, beat egg yolks until thick and lemon-colored. Beat in sugar gradually. Blend chocolate mixture into egg mixture. Set aside.

In a large bowl of an electric mixer, beat egg whites and cream of tartar until stiff. Carefully fold in egg yolk–chocolate mixture. Pour into soufflé dish. Set in a larger pan and pour in 1 inch hot water. Bake for 45–50 minutes, or until silver knife inserted in center comes out clean. Serve immediately on warm dessert plates. Top with whipped cream and toasted sliced almonds.

Serves 6–8

Cream Puffs

1 cup water
8 tablespoons (1 stick) unsalted butter,
        cut into pieces
½ teaspoon salt
1 cup sifted all-purpose flour
4 large eggs
1 large egg yolk
Ice cream, for serving
Confectioners' sugar, for serving (optional)

Heat oven to 400º.

In a medium heavy-bottomed saucepan over medium-high heat, bring water, butter, and salt to a boil. Reduce heat to low and add flour, beating vigorously with a stiff wire whisk or a wooden spoon until mixture leaves the sides of the pan and forms a ball. Remove from heat and transfer dough to the bowl of a stand mixer fitted with the paddle. Add eggs, one at a time, beating at high speed after each addition. Beat in the yolk last. Beat until dough is very smooth.

Drop dough onto an ungreased baking sheet, making 10 uniform mounds and spacing about 2 inches apart. Bake for 45–50 minutes, until puffed, golden brown, and dry. Allow puffs to cool slowly, away from any drafts.

Cut off tops with sharp knife. Scoop out soft dough, if desired. Fill with your favorite ice cream. Replace top. Sprinkle with confectioners' sugar, if desired. Serve cold.

Makes 10 cream puffs

VARIATIONS

Éclairs: Fill a pastry bag fitted with a plain tip with cream puff dough and pipe out 12 fingers, 4 inches long and 1 inch wide. Bake at 400° for 45–50 minutes, or until puffed, golden brown, and dry. Cool. Cut tops off with a sharp knife. Fill with Rich Custard Filling (recipe follows) and replace tops.

Petits Choux: Fill a pastry bag fitted with a star tip with cream puff dough and pipe into mounds the size of a walnut. Bake at 400° for 30 minutes, or until puffed, golden brown, and dry. Cool. Cut tops off with a sharp knife. Fill with Rich Custard Filling (recipe follows) and replace tops.

I usually fill a pastry bag fitted with a star tip and pipe about 1½ teaspoons cream puff dough uniformly onto a nonstick sheet. Puffs may be stuffed with finely diced chicken, turkey, shrimp, or tuna salad.

Rich Custard Filling

½ cup sugar
½ teaspoon salt
⅓ cup all-purpose flour
2 cups milk
4 egg yolks, beaten
2 teaspoons vanilla extract

In a saucepan, mix sugar, salt, and flour. Stir in milk. Cook over medium heat, stirring, until it boils. Boil for 1 minute. Remove from heat. Stir a little over half of this hot mixture into beaten eggs. Blend into hot mixture in saucepan. Return to heat and cook, stirring, until mixture thickens. Cool and blend in vanilla.

Crème Brûlée

This is one of many favorite desserts Mrs. Bush loves to serve to her friends and guests. This dish, like many other desserts, is presented to the head of the table for serving. Mrs. Bush cracks the hardened shell ceremoniously, in a precise yet practiced motion, and carefully plates the dessert. This is in contrast to President Bush (41), who digs out the Crème Brûlée with a serving spoon and calls out, "Say when."

12 egg yolks
½ cup superfine sugar
2 tablespoons cornstarch
3 cups heavy cream
2 teaspoons vanilla extract
⅓ cup brown sugar, packed

In a large mixing bowl, beat egg yolks, sugar, and cornstarch until very thick. Set aside.

In top of a double boiler over direct heat, scald cream. Pour scalded cream into beaten yolk mixture, whisking constantly. Stir in vanilla. Return to double boiler and cook over simmering water, stirring constantly, until mixture thickens, about 5 minutes. Transfer mixture into a glass serving dish. Chill completely.

A few minutes before serving time, heat broiler. Sprinkle top with brown sugar. Place under hot broiler until sugar melts and forms glaze, about 1 minute.

Serves 10–12

Note: Crème Brûlée may be prepared in individual dessert dishes. Brown sugar may also be omitted, with granulated sugar used instead. A portable torch will quickly caramelize sugar evenly and will give more browning effect. Also, the crème can be cooled and served over sweetened fresh or poached fruit in individual dessert dishes.

Crêpes Suzette

FOR CRÊPES

2 cups whole milk
4 tablespoons unsalted butter,
*   plus additional for pan*
3 eggs, slightly beaten
1 cup all-purpose flour
2 teaspoons baking powder
1 teaspoon salt
3 tablespoons sugar

FOR SAUCE

⅔ cup unsalted butter
4 tablespoons sugar
⅔ cup orange juice
½ teaspoon grated orange zest

TO FINISH

Cointreau or brandy, heated

For crêpes: In a saucepan over low heat, heat milk and butter. Remove from heat and allow to cool to room temperature. When cooled, beat in eggs, flour, baking powder, and salt until smooth. Strain through a fine-mesh strainer into a bowl and allow batter to rest for at least 1 hour. Batter should be at room temperature when cooking crêpes.

Prepare a shallow sheet pan by sprinkling with 3 tablespoons sugar. Set aside.

Fill a bowl to brim with cold water.

Heat a nonstick 6-inch skillet over medium-high heat until a drop of water sizzles and evaporates. Brush bottom of skillet lightly with butter. Spoon in 2 tablespoons batter and quickly tilt in all directions to coat bottom completely with the batter. Cook until edges begin to color, about 30 seconds. Edges will curl up; carefully lift an edge with a toothpick and grasp with your fingers; flip and cook the other side for 30 seconds. Invert skillet onto sugared pan. Keep crêpe flat. Dip bottom of skillet into the bowl with cool water. Repeat process until all the batter has been used. Greasing bottom of skillet may not be needed between cooking of crêpes.

Cover with damp clean towel to keep crêpes moist until ready to use (see Note).

This makes about 30 crêpes.

For sauce: In a heavy-bottomed saucepan over medium heat, melt butter. Add sugar, orange juice, and zest, stirring until sauce boils. This makes 1⅓ cups, enough for 4 servings.

To finish: Heat crêpes by flipping in hot saucepan, then fold them in halves or quarters. Place 4 on each dessert plate with some of the hot sauce spooned over. Serve at once.

To flame, arrange crêpes on a heatproof glass serving dish. Spoon on hot sauce. Pour either heated Cointreau or brandy over crêpes and light before serving. Crêpes are then passed around the table.

> *Note:* Crêpes may be prepared ahead of time and frozen for 2 months wrapped with plastic around sheet pan and towel. When ready to use, simply remove plastic and heat in oven, with the towel, for about 6 minutes. Remove from oven; allow crêpes to defrost at room temperature completely. Remove towel and carefully separate defrosted crêpes.

Esponjosa (Caramel Soufflé)

This Caramel Soufflé was the dessert served when Vice President and Mrs. Bush attended a luncheon at the residence of the CNO (Chief of Naval Operation), and Mrs. Bush asked for the recipe. I prepare this dessert to serve large groups of people at Walker's Point. The dining room seating capacity is forty-eight, but it can easily stretch to a hundred by extending table services out to the patio which overlooks the ocean. I serve one soufflé dish per table of twelve and have plenty of second helpings for everyone.

Doro, since childhood, never revealed which dessert she loved the most—unlike her four older siblings. She loved Pecan Pie just as much as Neil loves it, Baked Peaches Flambé as much as Jeb and George W., and Apple Betty and Apple Crisp just as much as Marvin. At the Vice President's House, she tasted the Caramel Soufflé, filled with assorted berries and topped with English Custard Sauce. It was love at first taste and has become her confirmed favorite ever since.

FOR CARAMEL BASE

1¼ cups superfine sugar

FOR MERINGUE

12 egg whites, at room temperature
2 cups superfine sugar

FOR CARAMEL CRUNCH

¾ cup superfine sugar

Fresh berries and sliced kiwis, for serving
English Custard Sauce (page 214), for serving (optional)

Heat oven to 250°.

For caramel base: In a heavy-bottomed saucepan or skillet over high heat, caramelize sugar until it begins to boil and turns medium brown. Remove from heat. Holding a 12-inch ring mold with hot pad, pour in hot caramel all at once. Tilt and rotate mold so caramel will cover bottom and sides. Use wooden spoon to spread caramel as high up the sides as possible. Set aside to cool. Caramel tends to crack as it cools.

For meringue: In the bowl of a stand mixer fitted with a whisk, beat egg whites at high speed until stiff, about 8 minutes. Reduce speed to low and slowly pour in 2 cups sugar.

Scrape sides of bowl with rubber spatula. Continue mixing at low speed for 3 minutes, scraping sides every minute. Set speed to high and continue beating for another 15 minutes.

For caramel crunch: Before beating time is up for egg whites, in a saucepan over high heat caramelize ¾ cup sugar until light to medium amber. (Do not burn, or caramel will give a bitter aftertaste to your soufflé.) Immediately place hot saucepan in cold water to cool for 1 second, until syrup thickens. Turn mixer to medium speed and in a steady stream pour syrup into beaten egg mixture, making sure that caramel does not fall on whisk. Return to high speed and beat for another 12 minutes. Mixture will now become cream-colored and glossier.

Transfer meringue into coated ring mold and fill all the way to the top. Run a knife through meringue to release air bubbles. Use all the egg mixture. There should be no meringue left in the mixing bowl. Set mold in large shallow pan. Pour in 1 inch boiling water. Bake 1 hour, until firm and soufflé has risen about 1½ inches above mold.

Remove soufflé from water bath and cool on rack before refrigerating for 6 hours or overnight. Soufflé will shrink when chilled.

To unmold, run a heated knife around edges of mold to loosen. Hold mold in pan of hot water for at least 3 minutes to warm syrup in bottom of mold. Invert on serving dish at least 1 inch larger than mold.

Fill center with fresh raspberries, blueberries, or strawberries. Decorate sides with more fruit slices. Kiwi slices may be used as mock leaves. Caramel syrup can be spooned over soufflé. Spoon off caramel syrup if soufflé is to be served with English Custard Sauce.

Serves 10–12

Herman's Floating Island

This recipe was shared by Herman Capati. He was the Master Chief Petty Officer Mess Specialist in charge of the household staff at the Vice President's House during Mr. Bush and Mr. Quayle's tenures. The finished product is as light as air—egg whites poached in milk and served floating on a light custard sauce and topped with caramel swirls.

FOR POACHING LIQUID

4 cups milk (low-fat or skim)
¾ cup sugar
1 vanilla bean, split in half lengthwise

FOR MERINGUES

8 egg whites, at room temperature
¼ cup sugar
Pinch of salt

FOR SAUCE

8 egg yolks
1⅓ cups sugar

FOR CARAMEL SWIRLS

¾ cup sugar
2 tablespoons water

For poaching liquid: In a large skillet, combine milk and sugar. Scrape seeds from vanilla bean and add seeds and pod to milk. Bring to a boil, stirring to dissolve sugar. Remove from heat and set aside.

For meringues: In the bowl of a stand mixer fitted with a whisk, beat egg whites, sugar, and salt until stiff and glossy.

Return skillet with poaching liquid to heat and heat liquid to 170°. Maintain that temperature while you poach the meringues. Discard vanilla bean pod.

Use a large cooking spoon to form 10 meringues. Drop meringues into barely simmering liquid and poach each side for 2 minutes, turning with a slotted spoon. With a slotted spoon, transfer meringues to a tray lined with paper towels. Set aside. Reserve poaching liquid.

For sauce: In a bowl, beat egg yolks and sugar until smooth. Strain poaching liquid into yolks, beating steadily. Pour into a saucepan. Cook, stirring, over low heat, until thickened. Remove from heat and set saucepan in a bowl of ice and stir until just warm. Strain sauce.

For caramel swirls: In a small heavy-bottomed saucepan over medium heat, caramelize sugar and water until medium amber. Let cool for 2 minutes.

To serve, fill dessert bowls half full with sauce. Set a meringue into each bowl. Dip a fork into the caramel and drizzle over meringues, to give the effect of candy swirls. Keep in a cool place until serving time (do not refrigerate).

Serves 10

Fruity Meringue Roll on Sabayon Sauce

> 4 egg whites
> 1 cup sugar
> 1 teaspoon cornstarch
> 1 cup heavy cream, whipped to stiff peaks
> 6 same-size strawberries
> ¼ ripe cantaloupe, peeled, seeded,
>   and cut into 4 pieces
> ¼ ripe honeydew, peeled, seeded,
>   and cut into 4 pieces
> 4 kiwifruit, peeled, cut in half
> 2 cups Sabayon Sauce (page 215)
> Confectioners' sugar, for serving (optional)

Heat oven to 350º. Spray a 13 x 9½-inch jelly-roll pan with pan spray and line pan with parchment. Spray parchment with pan spray. Have ready a kitchen towel sprinkled generously with sugar.

In the bowl of an electric mixer fitted with the whisk, beat egg whites and sugar until stiff and glossy. Strain cornstarch over egg whites and fold it in. Spread meringue evenly in jelly-roll pan. Bake for 20–25 minutes, until golden brown.

While still warm, turn pan over onto the sugar-dusted towel. Lift off pan, remove parchment, and cool meringue to room temperature.

Spread whipped cream evenly over meringue. With a short side of meringue facing you, arrange rows of strawberries, cantaloupe, honeydew, and kiwi fruit. Roll meringue

Fruity Meringue Roll on Sabayon Sauce

Executive Pastry Chef Roland Mesnier has always been accommodating to me each time I visit him in his workshop in the basement of the White House to watch him create whatever is on the menu that day. In my four years at the White House, I watched and learned from him, but the most amazing feats I've seen are his ways of turning basic recipes into astonishing finished products. Each presentation is always entirely different from another, no duplication, no recycling—always an original. *Dessert University*—the book he wrote with Lauren Chattman after retiring from the White House—says it all. He's the best of the best. He dedicated a copy of the book to President (41) and Mrs. Bush. It's the best gift one can ever receive. Every household should have a copy of his spectacular pastry recipes and essential lessons.

like a jelly roll, using the towel to guide cake into a firm, tight roll. Transfer roll to a platter and chill thoroughly.

To serve, spoon Sabayon Sauce onto dessert plates. Cut roll into 8 slices, and set slices upright on sauce. Dust with confectioners' sugar, if desired.

Serves 8

Baked Peaches Flambé

Mrs. Grace Walker shared this recipe with Mrs. Bush. It has been the favorite dessert of Florida's Governor John Ellis Bush and the 43rd President, George Walker Bush, since their childhood. No one can recall who was the first to claim this dessert as his very own favorite, so Mrs. Bush and Paula make sure it is offered every time either one of them comes to visit. According to Paula, when she or Mrs. Bush baked the peaches when the children were a lot younger, the aroma filled the house and gave rise to household jokes such as Jeb or George must have gotten good grades on their report cards, so they're having peaches—or won a game, or lost a tooth. When one of them comes home for a visit, the sweet peach aroma will still fill the air. The recipe is so simple and easy to prepare, but it's also elegant and very entertaining to serve. Mrs. Bush also added that Aunt Grace and Uncle Lou came over for dinner one night and were served the peaches for dessert. She asked Mrs. Bush wherever did she get this recipe—not remembering that she gave it to Mrs. Bush.

> 4 (29-ounce) cans peach halves, drained, liquid reserved
> 1 cup brown sugar, packed
> Juice of 1 lemon
> 2 tablespoons vanilla extract
> 1 cinnamon stick, broken in half
> 4 tablespoons unsalted butter, cut into small pieces
> ¼ cup brandy, heated
> Heavy cream, softly whipped, for serving

Heat oven to 250º.

Fill a 13 x 9-inch glass dish with peach halves, arranging them tightly, cut side up. Set aside. Add brown sugar to reserved peach liquid and stir until sugar dissolves. Stir in lemon juice and vanilla. Pour over peaches, and tuck in cinnamon. Top each peach half with a dab of butter. Bake for 1 hour, or until the liquid has reduced to a thick syrupy sauce. Allow peaches to cool to room temperature before serving.

Pour heated brandy over peaches and ignite with a match and present the dish to the head of the table while peaches are aflame. Provide serving spoons and dessert plates. The head of the table will serve the peaches (2 per serving) on dessert plates and drizzle the flaming syrup over the peaches. Pass whipped cream around to complement the peaches.

Serves 12

Note: Canned peaches tend to shrink during the hour-long baking, so I make a variation. I boil the reserved peach liquid in a medium saucepan with the sugar, lemon juice, and 1 tablespoon ground cinnamon until the liquid has turned into a thick and syrupy sauce and has reduced by half. I pour the syrup over the peaches, rearranging in neat rows, if needed. I top each peach with slices of butter and bake peaches for 30 minutes in a 375° oven. I occasionally use ¼ cup dark rum in place of the brandy for flaming.

Paula's Pears in Wine with Zabaglione Sauce

This is another recipe shared by Paula Rendon.

> 2 cups red wine
> 1⅓ cups granulated sugar
> 2 cinnamon sticks
> 10 whole cloves
> 2 cups canned Bartlett pear halves,
>   drained
> 6 egg yolks
> 1 cup white wine
> ⅓ cup brown sugar

In a medium saucepan, combine red wine, 1 cup sugar, cinnamon sticks, cloves, and pears. Bring to a simmer, and simmer for 15 minutes, covered. Remove from heat and allow to cool. Transfer pears, cut side up, to a serving bowl and refrigerate until ready to serve. Discard poaching mixture.

In top of a double boiler, whisk egg yolks and ⅓ cup sugar. Blend in white wine and cook over simmering water, stirring constantly, until sauce thickens.

Pour sauce over pears and sprinkle with brown sugar. Finish by placing under broiler and allowing brown sugar to caramelize, or use a portable torch for a quick caramelizing effect.

Serves 4

Meringue Bread Pudding

President Bush (41) asks for bread pudding once in a while. This is one of his favorites.

> 4 cups fine dry bread crumbs
> 6 cups scalded milk
> 2 large eggs plus 4 egg yolks, beaten
> ⅔ cup plus ¼ cup sugar
> 2 teaspoons vanilla extract
> Freshly grated nutmeg
> Currant jelly, melted
> 2 egg whites

Heat oven to 350°.

Place bread crumbs in an ungreased 3-quart baking dish.

In a large bowl blend milk, eggs and yolks, ⅔ cup sugar, and vanilla together. Pour over bread crumbs. Sprinkle with nutmeg. Place baking dish in a larger pan and pour in 1 inch hot water. Bake for 1 hour. Remove from oven.

Spread thin layer of currant jelly over bread pudding.

In a medium bowl, beat egg whites and ¼ cup sugar to soft peaks. Cover bread and jelly with meringue. Return to oven and bake for about 15 minutes, or until meringue is browned. Cool for 20–30 minutes before serving.

Serves 10–12

Raspberry Parfait

FOR BOTTOM LAYER

1 vanilla bean
1 large egg
1 egg yolk
1 cup honey
2 cups toasted almond halves

FOR SECOND LAYER

2 (6-ounce) baskets raspberries
2 cups sugar
4 egg whites
2 cups heavy cream
½ cup raspberry brandy

Line a 8 x 5-inch loaf pan with parchment.

For bottom layer: Cut vanilla bean in half lengthwise and scrape seeds from pod. Chop and pulverize pods and set aside. In top of a double boiler over simmering water, whip egg, egg yolk, honey, pulverized vanilla bean, and scraped seeds until thick. Remove from heat. Gradually fold in almonds. Put into loaf pan and freeze for at least 4 hours, until firm.

For second layer: Mash raspberries and push through a fine sieve; discard seeds. Transfer puree to a saucepan and boil with 1 cup sugar. Set aside to cool.

In a bowl, whip egg whites to soft peaks. Add 1 cup sugar and continue whipping until medium stiff.

During President Bush and Russian President Mikhail Gorbachev's meeting in Malta in December 1989, I was asked to prepare the meals for both entourages. I boarded the cruiser USS *Belknap* (CG-26), the flagship of the Sixth Fleet, in Valletta Harbor. Anchored about a mile away was the Soviet Cruiser *Slava*. Marine One flew in the President and his staff from USS *Forestall*, and they boarded the cruiser USS *Belknap*. President Bush spent time meeting the crew of the ship, and in the afternoon the President, Tim McBride, and I went fishing off the fantail of the cruiser. We didn't catch anything. The weather got worse, and no boats could take us back to the dock.

That same evening, the ship was rolling and tossing. The President, along with Secret Service details, were up in the bridge of the ship with Admiral Jonathan D. Williams, watching the swells of the ocean. The President looked down and saw a silhouette of someone over the bow of the ship. He seemed to be holding on to something—trying to keep his balance while looking down over the side of the ship. President Bush asked, "Why doesn't that guy get out of this awful weather and seek shelter?" The officer on duty at the bridge responded it was the sailor's duty to stand on watch at the bow to keep an eye on the lines and make sure the bobbing of the ship didn't drag the anchors and drift toward the dock. He was the telephone talker and the eye of the ship at the bow. The President, without warning, left the protection of the bridge; he got out in the open and, with steady sea legs, went to meet the telephone talker. He shook his hand and thanked him for helping keep the ship safe. Through strong blustery winds and blinding rain, the soaked agents who struggled behind the President saw the sailor's surprised eyes and his jaw drop in amazement.

The next day, the weather got worse, and dinner was canceled. President Gorbachev declined to come aboard the USS *Belknap*, where the dinner was to be held in the Officers' Wardroom. The menu included broiled swordfish, steamed Maine lobster, new potatoes, baby carrots, and a special dessert from Chef Roland Mesnier. I served the dinner to the President, Secretary of State James Baker, Dr. Burton P. Lee (the presidential physician), and Admiral J. D. Williams.

In another bowl, whisk cream until frothy. Fold whipped cream into whipped egg whites alternately with raspberry puree. Gently fold in raspberry brandy. Pour over bottom layer in loaf pan and freeze overnight.

Remove parfait from freezer 5 minutes before serving time. Unmold and slice into individual serving portions.

Serves 8

AFTERWORD

Whenever the President and First Lady visit various places, whether it's a private home in America or a destination around the world, their hosts and hostesses always provide the best entertainment and, most of all, the best and most sophisticated, elegant, and eye-catching menu items—all prepared by great chefs.

The collection of recipes was shared by friends of the Bush family and by chefs who, at one time or another, rendered their services at the White House, Camp David, the Vice President's House, Walker's Point, the Bush family's Houston residence, or at the Presidential Library in College Station, Texas.

These recipes may look familiar, but the difference is that all were tasted, sampled, and savored by two of our presidents and first ladies, vice presidents, foreign leaders, prime ministers, high officials, dignitaries, heads of state, kings and queens, princes and princesses, eminencies, lords, and magistrates alike!

It gives us all the wisdom and essence of gourmet dining in America. Enjoy!

ACKNOWLEDGMENTS

My warmest thanks to the following people for their support during the course of my military career and beyond, and as I wrote this book:

To my wife, Elizabeth, for her patience, affection, and devotion during my long absences from home and for her unwavering support of my collective work. Thank you for always being there for me and our family. To my sons, Ariel Cesar and Orville, and my son-in law, Lawrence—your input and technical support during production of this book were instrumental in its completion.

Special thanks to my daughter, Melody Cooper. Your ideas and long hours helping prepare this book for submission were invaluable.

My dad, Juanito, for encouraging me to write this book. To my dear mother, Guadalupe, whom I carry with me in spirit, thank you for watching over me and giving me strength to fulfill my destiny. To my brothers Celso, Eleazar, and Gamaliel, thank you for your support. To my youngest brother, Cesar, many thanks for cheering me on and constantly believing in me. To my sisters Naomi, Eduarda, Tessie, and Maggie, thanks for your encouragement.

To Terri Lacey and her husband, Jim Baird, for their tremendous and generous support of this book.

To former Navy Lieutenant Ray Cook, my Division Officer, onboard USS *Fairfax County* who insisted that I accept the job offer that essentially began my White House tour of duties.

To all my counterparts and mentors at the Vice President's House for sharing their immeasurable talents: Elias Rodriguez, Herman Capati, Romeo Cruz, Rudy Arca, Florencio Chan, Emil Edora, Angel Paraoan, Orlando Frilles, Danilo Ibanez, and Donald Burnside.

To my counterparts at the White House Mess who assisted me during numerous presidential trips across the country and around the world: Julian Almonte, Joven Fama, Fred Sanchez, Richard Sanvictores, Lito Bautista, Bayani Nelvis, Glen Maes, Robert Dempsey, Rusty Francisco, Willie Nocon, and Mike McGrath. To Alex

Layug, Fidel Medina, Tony Siack, Steve Boos, Robert Davila, John Palermo, and Dennis Laforteza for their assistance at Walker's Point during presidential visits.

Many thanks to Admiral John Stufflebeam for his support during key transitions in my naval and civilian careers. Admiral Stufflebeam was a Navy Commander and Military Aide to President George Bush when I first began working with him at the White House. To this day, his guidance and support serve as my major career highlights.

To the publishing staff members of Simon & Schuster and to the Scribner editorial and support staff. Thank you for your enthusiasm and extended efforts toward publishing my book.

At Scribner, special thanks to Lisa Drew, Samantha Martin, Susan Moldow, Roz Lippel, John Fulbrook, Mia Crowley-Hald, Erich Hobbing, Suzanne Balaban, and Erin Cox.

Special thanks to Roy Finamore for his masterful editing of my recipes.

Mark Thomas, talented photographer who captured gorgeous images throughout this book, working with food stylist William Smith and prop stylist Nancy Micklin. And to Chris and Cindy Smith of Ocean Exposure, C.A. Smith Photography.

To Bicker and Joyce Cain, for supporting me at the George Bush Library, Texas A&M University.

To Jean Becker for her moral support; Michele Whalen for her tireless research. And to the entire George Bush office staff for their support and encouragements.

Over the years I have had the great privilege of cooking for and meeting so many of the Bushes' many, many friends, but several stand out for their support: CBS sportscaster Jim Nantz, and the Oak Ridge Boys and their wives: Duane and Norah Lee Allen, Joe and Mary Bonsall, William Lee and Brenda Golden, and Richard and Donna Sterban. Thank you for your generous friendship and enthusiasm for what goes on in the kitchen.

To household staff members Paula Rendon, Alicia Huizar, and Teresa Martinez for assisting and working closely with me throughout our years at the Bush residences.

My thanks to President George W. Bush and First Lady Laura and to Governor Jeb and Columba, Neil and Maria, Marvin and Margaret, Doro Bush Koch and husband Robert and all their children, for accepting me as one of the family.

My thanks to William LeBlond and Sharon Bush for their friendship.

Ongoing thanks to former President George Herbert Walker Bush and former First Lady Barbara Pierce Bush. One can never find such a marvelous couple to serve. It continues to be an honor and a privilege to be a part of your family.

INDEX

adobo:
    chicken, 111–12
    pork, 134
    pork chops, 135
    pork spareribs, 134
aïoli, 198
almond(s):
    chicken, 112–13
    in chocolate meringue
      sundaes, 275–76
    pastry-wrapped Brie with,
      38–39
    velvet sauce, 203
appetizers:
    avocado dip, 30
    Beth's Philippine lumpia,
      42–43
    bologna roll, 49
    caviar croustades, 34
    cheese cups, 36
    cheese puff delights, 46
    Chinese egg rolls, 40–42
    clam dip, 29
    crab puffs, 45–46
    croustades (toast cups), 34
    crudités with curry dip,
      28–29
    Doro's Tex-Mex dip, 31
    empanadas, 44–45
    mushroom croustades,
      33–34
    mushroom quiches, 47–48
    pastry-wrapped Brie with
      almonds, 38–39
    pastry-wrapped pineapple
      cream cheese, 39–40

appetizers (*cont.*)
    sausage cheese balls, 48
    scallion-cheese squares,
      37
    shrimp and blue cheese
      croustades, 35
apple(s):
    Betty, 269
    crisp, 270
    in fabulous noodle kugel,
      124–25
    in Senegalese soup, 65
artichoke(s):
    citrus soup, 55
    stuffed, 179
asparagus:
    creamy, 180
    in seafood casserole,
      165–66
    tomatoes, shallots,
      pistachios and, 180–81
    in Walker's Point lobster
      salad, 162–63
avocado(s):
    dip, 30
    in Doro's Tex-Mex dip,
      31
    in frosty gazpacho, 53–54
    and hearts of palm salad, 75
    in pico de gallo, for tacos,
      129
    for Texas tortilla soup, 60
    in Walker's Point
      guacamole, 130
    in Walker's Point lobster
      salad, 162–63

bacon:
    in baked green beans,
      183–84
    in chaparral wilted spinach
      salad, 78
    in Cobb salad, 70
    in Jen's broccoli salad, 68
    in vegetable salad, 79
baked Alaska, 271–72
bamboo shoots:
    in almond chicken, 112–13
    in cashew chicken, 108–9
    in garlic chicken, 106–7
banana(s):
    bread, 224
    muffins, Walker's Point,
      222
barbecue sauce, Elizabeth's,
    204
bars, lemon, 262
basil, in pesto, 209
beans:
    red kidney, in empanadas,
      44–45
    refried, in Doro's Tex-Mex
      dip, 31
bean sprouts, in shrimp egg
    foo yong, 167
Béarnaise sauce, 198–99
beef:
    in empanadas, 44–45
    fajitas, 133
    mandarin orange, 122
    in meat sauce for tacos,
      126–27
    Mongolian, 116–17

marinades (*cont.*)

for Peking spareribs, 143–44

for pork tenderloin with mustard sauce, 141

for pork with scallions, 139

for sweet-and-sour pork, 136–37

for Walker's Point shish kebabs, 145

mayonnaise:

in curry dip, crudités with, 28–29

-dill sauce, poached salmon with, 154–55

in Grandmother Pierce's creamy salad ring, 71–72

in Jen's broccoli salad, 68

in mixed vegetable casserole, 196

in Spike's marinated swordfish, 159

in vegetable salad, 79

meats:

beef and pea pods, 118–19

beef fajitas, 133

beef fajitas buffet, 132

beef pepper steak, 120

in Beth's Philippine lumpia, 42–43

crispy pork, 140

curry-glazed pork chops, 142

mandarin orange beef, 122

marinated beef tenderloin, 123–24

marinated pork tenderloin with mustard sauce, 141

marinated pork with scallions, 139

Mongolian beef, 116–17

Peking spareribs, 143–44

pork adobo, 134

pork chops adobo, 135

pork spareribs adobo, 134

meats (*cont.*)

Prince Bandar's kapsa, 149

Prince Bandar's marak, 150

Prince Bandar's salsa, 151

rolled lamb divine, 146–47

sauce, for tacos, 126–27

sesame beef, 121

sweet-and-sour pork, 136–37

Taco Day buffet, 127

tacos, 126–32

Taiwanese barbecued pork, 138

Walker's Point shish kebabs, 145

meringues:

bread pudding, 289–90

for buttermilk layer cake with strawberry cream, 244–46

chocolate, sundaes, 275–76

fruity, roll on sabayon sauce, 285–87

Mongolian beef, 116–17

Mornay sauce, rich, 200–201

mousses:

for chocolate indulgence, 248–51

simple chocolate-coffee, 273

muffins:

blueberry crumb, 219

Walker's Point banana, 222

Walker's Point blueberry, 218

Walker's Point blueberry cornmeal, 220

Walker's Point strawberry, 221

mushrooms:

carrot-stuffed, 186–87

-cheese soufflé, 174

in chicken combo, 94–95

in chicken curry, 113

croustades, 33–34

quiches, 47–48

mushrooms (*cont.*)

in sauce chasseur, 99

in shrimp curry, 164–65

stuffed, 186

in stuffed chicken legs, 98–99

-tomato sauce, 210

mustard:

in baked green beans, 183–84

in bologna roll, 49

in Elizabeth's barbecue sauce, 204

in rolled lamb divine, 146

sauce, marinated pork tenderloin with, 141

Newburg, seafood, 168

noodle kugel, fabulous, 124–25

nutty chocolate chip cookies, 258–59

nutty rice pilaf, 267–68

nutty sugar cookies, 267

oatmeal:

in apple Betty, 269

in apple crisp, 270

in chocolate chip cookies, 257–58

lace cookies, 263

in nutty chocolate chip cookies, 258–59

olives:

kalamata, in chiffonade of spinach, 77

pimiento-stuffed, for cheese cups, 36

ripe, in Cobb salad, 70

ripe, in Doro's Tex-Mex dip, 31

ripe, in stuffed artichokes, 179

stuffed, hearts of palm and avocado salad, 75

stuffed green, in crab Louis, 85